ACTION RESEARCH FOR GENDER EQUITY

feminist educational thinking

Series Editors:
Kathleen Weiler, Tufts University, USA
Gaby Weiner, Umeå University, Sweden
Lyn Yates, La Trobe University, Australia

This authoritative series explores how theory/practice and the development of advanced ideas within feminism and education can be fused. The series aims to address the specific theoretical issues that confront feminist educators and to encourage both practitioner and academic debate.

Published titles:

Britt-Marie Berge with Hildur Ve: *Action Research for Gender Equity*
Jill Blackmore: *Troubling Women: Feminism, Leadership and Educational Change*
Jacky Brine: under*Educating Women: Globalizing Inequality*
Kaye Haw: *Educating Muslim Girls: Shifting Discourses*
Bob Lingard and Peter Douglas: *Men Engaging Feminisms*
Petra Munro: *Subject to Fiction: Women Teachers' Life History Narratives and the Cultural Politics of Resistance*
Kathleen Weiler and Sue Middleton (eds): *Telling Women's Lives*

ACTION RESEARCH FOR GENDER EQUITY

BRITT-MARIE BERGE
with
HILDUR VE

OPEN UNIVERSITY PRESS
Buckingham · Philadelphia

Open University Press
Celtic Court
22 Ballmoor
Buckingham
MK18 1XW

e-mail: enquiries@openup.co.uk
world wide web: http://www.openup.co.uk

and
325 Chestnut Street
Philadelphia, PA 19106, USA

First Published 2000

A catalogue record of this book is available from the British Library

ISBN   0 335 20022 2 (pb)   0 335 20023 0 (hb)

Library of Congress Cataloging-in-Publication Data
Berge, Britt-Marie, 1948–
     Action research for gender equity / Britt-Marie Berge with Hildur Ve.
        p.   cm. – (Feminist educational thinking)
     Includes bibliographical references and index.
     ISBN 0-335-20023-0. – ISBN 0-335-20022-2 (pbk.)
     1. Sex role – Study and teaching (Elementary) – Sweden.   2. Action research in education – Sweden.   I. Ve, Hildur.   II. Title.   III. Series.
HQ1075.5.S8B47   1999
306.7′071–dc21   99-16161
                                                                                                    CIP

Typeset by Type Study, Scarborough
Printed in Great Britain by Biddles Ltd, Guildford and King's Lynn

Contents

Series editors' preface

At the end of the twentieth century it is not a new idea to have a series on feminist educational thinking – feminist perspectives on educational theory, research, policy and practice have made a notable impact on these fields in the final decades of the century. But theory and practice have evolved, and educational and political contexts have changed. In contemporary educational policy debates, economic efficiency rather than social inequality is a key concern; what happens to boys is drawing more interest than what happens to girls; issues about cultural difference interrupt questions about gender; and new forms of theory challenge older frameworks of analysis. This series represents feminist educational thinking as it takes up these developments now.

Feminist educational thinking views the intersection of education and gender through a variety of lenses: it examines schools and universities as sites for the enacting of gender; it explores the ways in which conceptions of gender shape the provision of state-supported education; it highlights the resistances subordinated groups have developed around ideas of knowledge, power and learning; and it seeks to understand the relationship of education to gendered conceptions of citizenship, the family and the economy. Thus feminist educational thinking is fundamentally political; it fuses theory and practice in seeking to understand contemporary education with the aim of building a more just world for women and men. In so doing, it acknowledges the reality of multiple 'feminisms' and the intertwining of ethnicity, race and gender.

Feminist educational thinking is influenced both by developments in feminist theory more broadly and by the changing global educational landscape. In terms of theory, both post-structuralist and post-colonial theories have profoundly influenced what is conceived of as 'feminist'. As is true elsewhere, current feminist educational thinking takes as central the intersecting forces that shape the educational experiences of women and men. This emphasis on the construction and performances of gender through both discourses and material practices leads to an attitude of openness and questioning of accepted assumptions – including the underlying assumptions of the various strands of feminism.

In terms of the sites in which we work, feminist educational thinking increasingly addresses the impact of 'globalization' – the impact of neo-laissez-faire theories on education. As each of us knows all too well, the schools and universities in which we work have been profoundly affected by the growing dominance of ideas of social efficiency, market choice, and competition. In a rapidly changing world in which an ideology of profit has come to define all relationships, the question of gender is often lost, but in fact it is central to the way power is enacted in education as in society as a whole.

The books in this series thus seek to explore the ways in which theory and practice are interrelated. They introduce a third wave of feminist thinking in education, one that takes account of both global changes to the economy and politics, and changes in theorizing about that world. It is important to emphasize that feminist educational thinking not only shapes how we think about education but what we do *in* education – as teachers, academics, and citizens. Thus books within the series not only address the impact of global, national and local changes of education, but what specific space is available for feminists within education to mount a challenge to educational practices which encourage gendered and other forms of discriminatory practice.

Kathleen Weiler
Gaby Weiner
Lyn Yates

Preface

Action research has become popular in many countries particularly among teachers, education policy makers and politicians because it is concerned with researching practice for change. While action research has been strong on the practical application of research compared with other research approaches, it has been relatively weak in developing theoretical or critical perspectives. Moreover, action research studies have tended to be localized and specific, having little generalizable value. However, this book avoids such pitfalls. It works with a sharper version of action research that is more politically aware, better contextualized and cognisant of the partiality and specificity of action research accounts. In consciously seeking to avoid the criticisms of action research as above, Britt-Marie Berge and Hildur Ve have produced a lucid, thoughtful and accessible account of an action research project, which seeks to transcend national boundaries and specific school cultures.

Thus the authors offer an account of a unique attempt in one school in one country at a specific time to introduce change into the classroom: one which involves teachers, students and university researchers onstage; with parents, the Swedish state and policy makers backstage. All these individuals and institutions have an interest, in one way or another, in the process of challenging gender divisions in schools and in reflecting on the process. The account offered is thus, in one sense, specific to the circumstances of the school involved; yet in another, generative and generalizable to other times and places.

In terms of its contribution to the study of gender in schools, the book introduces two impotant new concepts: 'moments of normalization' which signal resistances to changed gender practices and relationships; and 'moments of equity' when recognizable progress towards gender equity is visible. These two concepts, in my view, will prove to be both illuminating and useful to other action and/or gender researchers as they seek to capture instances of gender advancement or retreat.

Finally, in its attempt to weave in all the stories of all the paricipants involved in the project, the book offers an original and accessible account of how classroom and practitioner research is possible, yet also alerts the reader to the snares and obstacles awaiting the unprepared and unwary researcher: for example, in relation to synthesizing differing points of view and value systems, differing power relationships and interests and differing perceptions of what is happening and what is being achieved.

For all these reasons and more, I am delighted to have this book in the series *feminist educational thinking* not only as a welcome broadening of the series' knowledge base and orientation towards practice and equity, but also as a significant contribution to educational action research more generally.

Gaby Weiner

1 Introduction

This book is about action research as a method for change and as a means of taking up feminist research in education. The book is written for practitioners and academics using action research and/or developing a feminist approach to pedagogy, teacher education and action research. We write this book in a (for us) foreign language, so as to make contact with readers from other countries and other school arenas where action research and the struggle for change take place. We argue that the way in which individuals struggle for change and the often contradictory way individuals react – supportive or resistant – to these struggles could be understood as unique to a given context but also connected to other similar contexts.

The book is both empirical and reflective. The main aim is to offer a new analysis of how equality strategies and policies are experienced in the classroom, drawing on mainly feminist poststructural theories. The design of the project and the collaboration between university staff, schoolteachers and school pupils are grounded in these frameworks. The book draws on two concepts in particular: *moments of equity* and *moments of normalization*. These concepts have been used in the project to highlight the contradictory and complex interplay of backlash against change and progress towards change in the action research process. What we mean by 'moments' is illuminating occasions when backlash or progress is visible.

We identify moments of normalization because, in showing resistance, they gave us a greater understanding of the gendered context of the classrooms. We used the term 'normalization' when the male or 'masculinity' was regarded as the inevitably regulative or superior norm, although people in everyday life may interpret 'normal' as something good and desirable. We regard moments of normalization as moments of backlash: moments when goals of equity are rejected. By being conscious of how these normalizing moments occur, teachers are more able to use purposeful and nuanced equality strategies to overcome them. A moment of equity occurs when someone identifies that progress is recognizably being made, or when equity is present.

This book provides a story of an attempt in Sweden to change the peda-gogical practices of five female and four male compulsory school teachers and their 120 pupils aged from 8 to 13 years. These teachers had been working with gender equality strategies for three years when we – Britt-Marie Berge, from Umeå University, Sweden, and Hildur Ve, from Bergen, Norway – were asked by the teachers to join them in an action research project for three further years. We planned the project together with the Swedish teachers, and during our joint work Britt-Marie Berge had the main responsibility for con-tacts with pupils and teachers and for data collection, while Hildur Ve was a consulting researcher. Grants were obtained mainly from the Swedish National Agency of Education and the local authority. The teachers have documented their work and experiences from our joint work in a report writ-ten for other teachers in Sweden. Since we have an agreement that the teachers should remain anonymous in work done by us, neither the title of this report, which consists the name of the school, nor the teachers' real names are given in this book. We call the report 'teachers' report' when we refer to it.

Britt-Marie Berge is responsible for most of the text in this book, except for Chapter 3, which is jointly written by Hildur Ve and Britt-Marie Berge. However, for stylistic purposes 'we' is used all through the book to denote the authors' voice.

In Chapter 2, the method and framework within which the teachers addressed problems of curricula and gender are presented. Chapter 3 con-sists of theoretical reflections. We start with a short sketch of the various stages through which our research projects have developed. We then discuss in more detail those theories that have served as our source of inspiration. Later, we discuss some critical approaches to these, before concluding with a kind of synthesis of our perspective.

In Chapter 4 some selected empirical examples of *moments of normaliza-tion* are presented. These examples refer to resistance to the goals of gender equity, not only among the pupils but also among the adults in the project. In Chapters 5, 6, and 7, we enter the six different classrooms. The main focus of these chapters is the presentation of teachers' and pupils' interpre-tations of when moments of equity are prevalent and their ideas on how to reach the aims of equity in school as well as in a future society. In Chapter 8, both theory and methodology in our project are reflected upon, in order to explore both the possibilities and the difficulties of action research pro-jects that attempt to promote gender equity in a society caught between the modern and the postmodern.

Action research and teaching for gender equality

Most approaches within education characterized as action research can be categorized as either 'teachers as researchers' or 'reflective practitioners' on the one hand, or 'critical praxis' aiming at emancipation on the other. Critical praxis regarding gender and education is relatively rare (Weiner 1989, 1997). Ulla Forsberg analysed the literature on school-based critical praxis projects focusing on gender published during the past ten years and available through university library databases (Forsberg 1998). By the time our project started she had found, in addition to Ve's Norwegian project, eight published reports regarding projects aimed at gender equality strategies in school (Chisholm and Holland 1986; Westblade and Miller-Kenneth 1989; Tutchell 1990; Weiner 1990; Leeming 1991; Neal 1991; Nicholas 1991; Kruse 1992). After our project had started, information on a further nine projects became available (Björkly and Hernes 1993; Griffiths and Davies 1993; Olafsdottir 1993; Frith and Mahony 1994; Kochenberger-Stroeher 1994; Arnesen 1995; Parker and Rennie 1995; Tuulenkari 1995; Freeman 1996).

These projects are spread throughout the world, with reports from Australia, Canada, the USA and Europe. From the number of publications emanating from the UK (eight), it appears that action research has had the greatest impact there. However, all these projects seem to be involved in different kinds of network with other schools working with these issues. We can therefore assume that there is more work going on in schools than is visible in databases of publications. In Sweden and Norway, for example, teachers very seldom document and report their work in published form.

These reported projects differ in design and dimension, and have been more or less closely connected to a university or to a school of education. Some projects lay particular stress on mapping and/or evaluation (Chisholm and Holland 1986; Westblade and Miller-Kenneth 1989; Kochenberger-Stroeher 1994; Parker and Rennie 1995), while others are devoted to the presentation of classroom practices (Tutchell 1990; Neal 1991; Björkly and Hernes 1993; Olafsdottir 1993; Tuulenkari 1995). Yet others contain an interaction of data collection with the evaluation and development of classroom practices (Weiner 1990; Leeming 1991; Nicholas 1991; Kruse 1992; Ve 1992; Griffiths and Davies 1993; Frith and Mahony 1994; Freeman 1996).

According to Forsberg, about half of these projects have a liberal feminist orientation to changing traditional gender patterns. These projects are devoted to creating as similar conditions as possible for each sex. To help students to cross traditional gender boundaries in choice of education and occupation, the projects try to change girls' and boys' attitudes and behaviour. Another way of working is to provide equal amounts of time for work with traditional masculine (most often) or feminine activities or tools.

Other projects have a more radical feminist approach, with a focus on differences between the sexes and their conditions and competences. These projects aim at radical changes in positions of power, and most projects are devoted to consciousness raising and to strengthening girls' self-reliance.

The issues are about highlighting girls and their competences and conditions: unequal power relations and sexism, for example. Single-sex groups are often used.

The outcome of the projects is that the teachers have learnt more about gender relations, and realize that gender issues are more complicated and teaching for gender equity is more difficult than at first thought. The children have become more aware of gender questions, and there are some reports that boys are not as hostile as before and there are some other changes in stereotypical gender patterns. However, the results are contradictory, and even if boys are reported to be less hostile in some cases and some changes in stereotypical gender patterns have been observed, there are either no reports or contradictory results regarding moments of real change in power positions between the sexes in local classrooms. On the whole, analyses of how gender is constructed and how individuals are positioned or position themselves during processes of action research in classrooms are conspicuously absent.

In a recent published international volume on action research and educational reform (Hollingsworth 1997), the contributors discuss action research as a research methodology. Susan Noffke and Marie Brennan (1997), for example, suggest in their article an improved version of action research, with greater political awareness, attention to contextual circumstances and recognition of the partiality and the specifics of history. They refer to work done by feminist researchers, such as the feminist post-colonialist theorist Spivak, suggesting that such research should also include the identification of sites and their connection to one another. Such strategies are highly relevant to action research, since it is possible to read the context more carefully and to analyse connections between arenas of practices, so that the local is not seen as separate from the global (Noffke and Brennan 1997: 67).

What is new about the project presented in this book is that we have worked with this improved version of action research. We recognize that the contradictions in the results presented in earlier work are due to the 'normal' contradictory processes which occur when people try to change power relations in, for example, classrooms. An awareness of these processes is necessary for any impact or enduring changes of power. As mentioned above, we present these contradictions with the help of the concepts 'moments of normalization' and 'moments of equity', and show with examples how the teachers tried to overcome the normalizing processes.

In this action research project we have focused on: (a) teachers' teaching; (b) girls' and boys' perceptions and experiences of teachers' teaching; and (c) gender relations in specific classroom contexts. One intention has been to analyse whether and how normalizing and regulative aspects of dominant discourses operate to subvert equity pedagogy. Another intention has been to deepen the understanding of different voices as a basis for action and change. The processes through which gender is constituted are discussed from a feminist poststructuralist and pragmatic perspective. Poststructuralism recognizes how power is contextually and discursively exercised at local levels and how it imbues people's thoughts and bodies. Within the same framework, feminist poststructuralism highlights how individuals actively position themselves in order to attain the object of their desires in the specific context: for example, equal relationships in the everyday world. There are some possibilities for individuals, through critical thinking, to resist, and even to some extent deconstruct and change, contextual gender power relations at local levels: for example, in classrooms.

Throughout the project, the teachers, pupils and researchers experienced both a desire for and a fear of change. We argue that an awareness of the different and often competing ways of giving meaning to practices will enable critical thinking about how power rules in one's own body and mind. This self-consciousness is a prerequisite for developing deconstructive strategies and finding ways of working with pedagogy to provide greater equity between the sexes. During this process the teachers have challenged not only the girls' but also the boys' ways of relating to individuals, education and society.

Since an awareness of contextual circumstances is necessary for understanding the examples, we continue with a brief overview of education in Sweden. We also include some more detailed statistics in Appendix 1.

The Swedish context

'Deregulation', 'privatization', 'decentralization' and an 'extremely wasteful public sector' are keywords in recent Swedish political rhetoric. These words are used by politicians on the right and the centre (including the ruling Social Democrats) in their attempts to drive change towards more direction by market forces and less state regulation. This so-called 'system shift' started at the end of the 1970s and was justified by the need to counteract the recession in Sweden. During this period Sweden entered the European Union and the government reorganized the economy according to EU demands, which implied a reduction in state subsidies. Benefits have slowly declined, resulting in cuts in state subsidies and the welfare state. The core of the Swedish state feminist approach to gender equality has been the promotion of parenting *and* paid employment for both women and men. For example, one way of working towards those aims has been to use the public sector as a promoter of both family services and employment opportunities, especially for women. However, because of recent economic politics the public sector has been shrinking (Oláh 1998).

Over the past three decades school policies have shifted from a centralized system, including regulated national curricula, towards decentralization, including goal-oriented national curricula. The most important aim of the previous centralized system was to guarantee an equal educational standard throughout the country. The arguments for the shift have focused on overcoming the negative aspects of too much state regulation of teachers' work and delegating more professional power to teachers. With the new goal-oriented national curricula, with less regulated timetables, schools can differ more than before. From now on teachers in each school can choose what they regard as the best ways to reach national goals in their classrooms. The debate has also focused on how to make schools more effective in reaching the aims of compulsory schooling and on how to 'measure' efficiency. National steering and control of compulsory schooling presupposes that, although schools have the same goals to achieve, they will have to perform different kinds of evaluations and follow-ups (Berge 1997: 7).[1]

The rhetoric of gender equality

Jämställdhet: *the Swedish word for gender equality*

The Swedish word for equality – *jämlikhet* – refers to equitable relations between all individuals and groups in society, and is based on the notion that all people are of equal value, regardless of sex, race, religion, ethnic origin or social class. However, when feminists in high positions in the Swedish state during the 1960s wanted to change unequal power relations between the sexes, they found that the word *jämlikhet* was a political embarrassment and a handicap to them. *Likhet* is a part of the word and carries an underlying notion of 'the same nature/looking alike'. Feminists feared that the word could have too many sexual undertones to be generally accepted in Sweden.

According to Florin and Nilsson (1997: 2), the feminists wanted to find a word as functional as the one used to describe the concept of the Swedish welfare state – *folkhemmet* – which literally means 'people's home'. *Folkhemmet* has no sexual undertones; it bridges class distinctions, sounds unthreatening and disguises underlying conflicts. State feminists chose the word *jämställdhet*, which is impossible to translate into English. Its meaning is 'women and men stand side by side in life'. The quantitative aspect of *jämställdhet* implies an equitable distribution of women and men in all areas and at all levels of society. If there is more than 60 per cent of one of the sexes there is no *jämställdhet*. The qualitative aspect implies that the different knowledge, experiences and values of women and men are used to enrich and direct all social areas and endeavours. During the 1970s the concept was introduced into politics by the Social Democrats and a State Delegation for Gender Equality was founded, which was to work to implement gender equality in Swedish society.

The rhetoric of policy

The rhetoric concerning gender equality was incorporated into Swedish legislation. During the 1980s gender equality had meant that women and men should have equal rights, but also equal responsibilities and opportunities in paid work, unpaid caring work and domestic work, and participation in politics, unions and other social activities (Swedish Government Bill 1987/8: 105: 3). In order to fulfil these aims in the three different areas and in accordance with the statistics on gender structure in Sweden at that time, men needed to participate more in unpaid work and women needed to participate more in paid work and politics. During the 1990s Government Bills stressed equal rights, responsibilities and opportunities for the sexes in *all* areas. The change in rhetoric towards the more common word 'all' is simultaneously a reinforcement and a weakening of the aims of gender equality, since it means everything but does not stress anything.

Swedish legislation regarding gender

During the 1990s neither the Gender Equality Act nor the Education Act had paragraphs covering all three areas. Only paid work is regulated in the Gender Equality Act, meaning that there are no regulations regarding the sexes and unpaid work. However, according to paragraph 5, the employer shall facilitate the combination of paid work and parenthood for both female and male employees. According to the Education Act, 'All children and youths shall, independent of sex, geographical domicile and social and economical conditions, have equal access to public education for children and youth' (Education Act 1996/7: 2). The word *jämställdhet* only appears in the Education Act in the middle of the 1990s. 'Those who work at school should promote equality between the sexes' (*ibid.*). In the rhetoric of the Swedish Government Bill of 1994/5 there are no explicit discussions concerning boys and their knowledge of care work and domestic work, though paid work and higher education, especially the need to get girls interested in natural sciences and technology, including data communication with computers, are highlighted.

The national curricula for compulsory schooling

The first two national curricula for the nine years of compulsory schooling (Läroplan för grundskolan 1962, 1969) were implemented after the Second World War under Social Democrat governments. In accordance with the gender equality aims, the curricula explicitly stressed the idea that old gender patterns should be challenged in compulsory education regarding both paid and unpaid work. Not only should girls and women change and enter male-dominated areas, but boys and men should also change and take more responsibility for unpaid care work and domestic work. In the same year that the first national curriculum became valid, home economics became a compulsory subject for both girls and boys and a new subject – the study of children and childhood – was introduced. In 1969, the two subjects textile craft and wood and metalwork were combined into one subject – craft – for both girls and boys (Berge 1992).

However, simultaneously with the introduction into the rhetoric of the concept *jämställdhet*, school policies changed. Subsequent national curricula became goal-oriented. This means that goals for educational attainment are set nationally, but the means of reaching these goals are left for teachers and schools to determine. The first goal-oriented curriculum was implemented by a non-socialist government, but the shift was continued and completed by the following Social Democrat governments.[2] The paradox during this period was that, just as the word *jämställdhet* entered the goal-oriented rhetoric to highlight gender equality, explicit demands regarding men's responsibilities in unpaid domestic work disappeared, while the need to encourage girls to enter into higher education and into paid work – especially in traditional male areas – was stressed.

It could be argued that the need to change men's gender patterns is implicit in the core of the *jämställdhet* concept. However, practices in school policies are inconsistent with that argument, since subjects connected with domestic knowledge have lost ground. In 1994 the 'study of children and childhood' disappeared as a specific subject and the time given to compulsory home economics was reduced. The only subject that has not lost ground is craft, a combined unit of traditional male and female subjects. In arguments for the importance of craft, its connections to technology, art and design have been highlighted, while connections to home economics are rarely made (Berge 1992).

One may, of course, argue that there are possibilities in the goal-oriented curricula and school policies for individual schools to create their own policies, stressing, for example, the importance of unpaid work and focusing especially on the need for boys to achieve such competence. But apart from some efforts in that direction in the project presented in this book, we know of no such school profiles in Sweden. The most common trends have been to highlight technology and data communication, often referring to the explicit rhetoric about gender equality and girls' needs in the national curriculum documents.

To sum up, even if nowadays there are no explicit obstacles for teachers to concentrate on in prioritizing the creation of gender equity, and even if the word for gender equity is used in the rhetoric of educational policy documents, subjects that are important for boys and gender equity have lost ground. That means that parental nurture is a high priority for neither boys nor girls. On the contrary, the rhetoric of gender equity for girls often points to girls fitting themselves to male-dominated fields of the labour market.

School context and teachers' work

Compulsory education consists in Sweden of nine years of schooling. When this project was carried out, children normally began school at the age of 7 and only 8 per cent of all pupils in the first grade were 6 years old.[3] There were three different categories of teachers working in three levels of school. Both junior level teachers in grades 1–3 (7–9 age group) and intermediate teachers in grades 4–6 (10–12 age group) were class teachers in almost all subjects. At the upper level in grades 7–9 (13–15 age group), subject teachers were teaching one or more subjects.[4]

Education policy and control of compulsory schools

When the action research project started, contradictions and tensions became obvious between the way practices of schooling developed in the research project and the way in which the implementation of the new national curriculum was being carried out at this school and other schools in Sweden.

As the teachers in this project developed their pedagogy, they looked upon the aims of the national curriculum as no more than general outlines. The teachers were aided by their visions of what the aims should mean in reality. It was the teachers, with their special competences, who had the freedom to choose content and methods to attain the aims. New ideas and teaching approaches often developed through everyday work with different pupils in different educational situations. Teachers felt that it was not possible to plan too much in advance if they wanted to address their pupils' needs in different educational situations (Tiller 1986). The most important tools in attaining national aims were the teachers themselves: their level of professionalism in reflecting on and challenging their own teaching when developing pedagogy in practice (Tabachnick and Zeichner 1991; Ladson-Billings 1994).

Despite the introduction of decentralization, local responsibility and aim-governed curricula, the teachers said they felt more directed at that time than during the earlier period of centralization. The action research project, according to the teachers, produced opportunities for greater freedom and possibilities to develop their professionalism. Similar tensions between action research and government education policy can be found in England (Weiner 1998) and Norway (Ve 1995). Noffke (1997) shows that similar contradictions between what she calls democracy and social engineering appeared within action research projects in the USA.

Local school context

Three female junior-level teachers, and two female and four male intermediate-level teachers participated in the project, as well as about 120 pupils in three classes from junior level and three classes from intermediate level.

The project was based in a Swedish school in a district with about 8500 inhabitants, near a town where most people work in administration, education, medical and other service occupations. The majority of the project teachers both lived and worked in the district. In the district, as well as in the whole authority, the average age of the population is fairly low – about 35 years – and the educational attainment – 82 per cent of females and 79 per cent of males completed higher education or upper secondary education – slightly higher than the average for the whole population in Sweden. About 6 per cent of the inhabitants in the district were born abroad or have not become Swedish subjects. In the six project classes only two pupils were black, and only one had parents born abroad.

About 80 per cent of the pupils lived in self-contained houses and just 2 per cent had a single parent, compared with 5 per cent in the whole country. In terms of the overall population in the district, 87 per cent of the population were in employment: 35 per cent worked in the district, 61 per cent in the nearby town and the rest in other local areas; 40 per cent of the jobs were in the industrial sector, 30 per cent in the public sector and 12 per cent in agriculture and forestry.[5] The majority of the pupils in the 'case study school' come from white middle-class and lower middle-class families. Those involved in the project school consequently represent white and fairly well educated Swedes living in nuclear families. (Other information on Sweden is provided in Appendix 1.)

Summary

In this chapter we have introduced the outline of this book and of the action research project carried out in Sweden. We have presented literature that is available about other school-based action research projects during the past ten years and briefly introduced the two concepts 'moments of normalization' and 'moments of equity', which have helped us to offer a new analysis of how equality strategies are experienced in action research in the classroom. To bring to the reader an awareness of the Swedish context, we have finally given a brief overview of education in Sweden.

Notes

1 Ve (1998) describes similar trends in Norway and Slee *et al.* (1998) in Britain.
2 Agreement between social democrats and non-socialist parties is visible in UK (Weiner 1998) and in Norway (Ve 1998).
3 As from 1 July 1991, parents can decide whether their child starts at 6 or 7.
4 After 1991/2 all compulsory school teachers have become educated as subject teachers teaching grades 1–7 or 4–9.
5 According to information from the district authority (1996).

2   A journey towards gender equity

In this chapter we describe how we worked with teachers on the gender equity project. In some respects doing action research is like travelling on an unspecified journey. Rather than following established routes, you create spaces and new directions while you are travelling. The only things known are the purpose for the journey and where and how to start. This chapter starts with a description of our point of departure, the vision of our final destination and our relationships. Then we present a clarification of some terms and meanings, ending with a description of process methods. But first a short flashback.

In 1990, one of the junior-level teachers, Eva, started to separate the pupils into single-sex groups for approximately a quarter of the total class time. Eva's main reason for separating the pupils was her experience that the boys dominated the classroom. She wanted to challenge the boys' domination and to strengthen the girls' position. She persuaded colleagues to join her in this work, although not all of them shared her experience of the boys consistently dominating the classroom. However, they were all interested in working for equity and social justice, and they regarded gender equity as a central element of that work. After three years the teachers were uncertain about what impact their work was having and how they should continue. They initiated a cooperative arrangement with us because they wanted to get feedback on their work and supportive discussion partners to help to develop their pedagogy further. Together with the teachers and the female director of this school, we jointly planned a three year cooperative action research project.

Point of departure

The passengers on this journey were us (two female researchers), five female and four male teachers and their 120 pupils at junior and intermediate levels of a compulsory school in Sweden. (See also 'School context and teachers' work in Chapter 1.)

Table 2.1 shows the six class teachers and the other teachers who took lessons in their classrooms. Eva, Lina and Lisbeth were the junior-level class teachers, teaching pupils aged 7–9 in grades 1–3. As well as being responsible for the teaching in their own classes, Eva was responsible for creative activities, Lina for technology and Lisbeth for care work in all three grade 1–3 classes participating in the project. Some of the juniors also took part in a music project with Viktor. The other teachers were teaching pupils aged 10 to 12 at intermediate level. Helena was used to taking over Eva's pupils, Siv was used to taking over Lina's pupils and Anders was used to taking over Lisbeth's pupils. Pupils at intermediate level also met other teachers. During the project Viktor taught music and Valdemar taught craft. Lars was a temporary teacher and besides teaching home economics he also shared the responsibility for natural science, English and Swedish together the three class teachers at intermediate level.

When the teacher/researcher cooperation was initiated, we all agreed that we should work on equal terms, contributing with different but equal competences and experiences. We, as researchers, should provide an outsiders'

Table 2.1 The six class teachers (shown in bold type) and other teachers taking lessons in their classrooms

Junior level, grades 1–3 *(7–9 years old)*	*Intermediate level, grades 4–6* *(10–12 years old)*

Eva
Viktor (music)
Lina (technology)
Lisbeth (care work)
	Helena
	Viktor (music)
	Lars (home economics, natural sciences,
	    English, Swedish)
	Valdemar (craft)
	(Helena and Siv mix their pupils for some
	    lessons)

Lina
Viktor (music)
Eva (creative activities)
Lisbeth (care work)
	Siv
	Viktor (music)
	Lars (home economics, natural sciences,
	    English, Swedish)
	Valdemar (craft)
	(Siv and Helena mix their pupils for some
	    lessons)

Lisbeth Viktor (music) Eva (creative activities) Lina (technology)	**Anders** Viktor (music) Lars (home economics, natural sciences, English, Swedish) Valdemar (craft)

views of educational situations and experiences from research, and hold the main responsibility for data collection from the classrooms, the design of which we always discussed with the teachers. Our main task when interpreting data was to look for normalizing (see Chapter 1) tendencies in the classrooms in order to take progressive steps. The teachers were to provide their professional insider knowledge of the specific context in discussions of how data should be interpreted and analysed. Another important task was to use their professionalism to create progressive teaching for greater equity in the classrooms. We decided that the third year should be devoted to careful consideration and documentation, because the oldest pupils were to be transferred to upper-level school and other teachers. We decided to write two reports. The first should be the teachers' story of the process and how they struggled to reach gender equity; the second should be our story of the process of action research for gender equity.

We jointly decided to develop the project by bringing in pupils' voices and emphasizing pupils' experiences. The method focused on pupils' vision of 'the good life' and of what equity meant to them currently as well as in the future, in school as well as in society. We tried to emphasize personal viewpoints rather than revealing personal histories. But we are aware that this is a difficult balancing act. The pupils' written documents are therefore anonymous. Our decision to include pupils' voices was the result of other action researchers' experiences. When we planned the project, we had just finished a Norwegian action research project concerning gender equity at the junior level in some compulsory schools in Norway (Ve 1992). The final evaluation stated that the effects of action research might have been greatly enhanced if the pupils had been drawn more actively into the project. Similar experiences have been reported by Ruth Frith and Pat Mahony (1994: 109) in the Gender Action Project (GAP) in the UK. They argue that many action research initiatives fail because they ignore pupils' perceptions and experiences of power, sexism and racism. Ignoring the pupils' experiences, teachers lack both insight into and knowledge of what fundamental changes must take place in order to attain more equitable relationships in the classroom.

Parents were informed of the project at a specially convened meeting. To get feedback and to let everyone put questions to the teachers, small group discussions followed the initial provision of information. During these group discussions, parents proved very supportive. Perhaps this could be explained by the fact that parents were already familiar with the issues, since the teachers had been working on these issues for the past three years. Those parents who had initially been hesitant had time to think and to discuss with the children and the teachers what was going on at school. None had any objections to having a researcher collecting data in the classrooms.

The Swedish school year is divided into two semesters. The project group met for four whole days every semester for discussion of the data and future action. We jointly decided, from time to time and from the teachers' needs, how best to use these days. Each day usually had one lecture by us or by someone invited, on a theme chosen by the teachers. The rest of the time was spent on discussion of how to interpret data and what equality strategies to use in the classroom practices. In addition to these days, the teachers decided to meet every Tuesday after school hours, to exchange experiences from the different classrooms, to discuss articles and books and to work together on practical arrangements. At first one of the researchers joined the Tuesday meetings. However, after some time we found that the most appropriate way of working was to have periods of intense teacher–researcher cooperation and periods of separation when we worked alone or in spontaneously formed smaller groups. The teachers were granted a reduction of one teaching hour every week while working with the project, and they could leave their classes in the charge of other teachers when they had to attend project meetings. Of course, more time than that was spent on the project.

In order to benefit from the experiences of other schools working on improving equality strategies in classrooms, the teachers joined the Swedish Jämsam network and the Nordic NordLilia network, and later they became involved in wider European networks. Project participants also visited teachers working with action research in schools connected to the University of Wisconsin in the USA.

We learnt from other action research projects that keeping diaries is a fruitful method of noting experiences (see, for example, Tiller 1986; Elliott 1991; Altrichter 1993). It was decided that project participants should keep diaries during the project. However, some teachers felt uncomfortable about letting other people read their diaries. We therefore decided that the diaries should be kept private. Each person could decide what, when and how information from the diary should be communicated to others. Some teachers, who experienced problems expressing themselves in written words, compiled their diaries in the form of photo albums, with short written comments alongside the photographs.

When we planned the project we were particularly interested in doing action research aiming at emancipation. At that time we were most familiar with the work of Kurt Lewin (1948), who is often presented as the father of action research (see, for example, Adelman 1993). We were above all attracted to and inspired by his optimistic view and his conviction that it was possible for subordinated peoples to break asymmetric power relations. The means to gain power are, according to Lewin, to reflect on and to capture knowledge about those situations where people become subordinated, to have joint discussions, to come to a joint decision on what to do and finally to carry that action through. A spiral is a useful metaphor to describe the different steps in the action research process: problem formulation, data collection, analysis of data, planning and realization of an action. Analysis and evaluation of the action raises new questions, demanding new investigations, new actions, new analysis and evaluations, which raise new questions and so on. Theories and conceptions relevant to the context are simultaneously introduced and developed. This way of working presupposes groups without any hierarchies. Lewin summarized the method as: no action without research and no research without action (Adelman 1993: 8).

The vision of our destination

The following conceptualizations of equity were regarded as key to the project. In the short term, the teachers tried to create an atmosphere where both girls and boys were seen and heard without being obstructed in any way. In the long-term perspective the teachers wanted to make a closer connection to the pupils' future lives as grown-up women and men, and to challenge what is often taken for granted, namely that in order for women to be active and adequate citizens they must act like men (Pateman 1989: 14). The teachers agreed with the official Swedish definition of gender equity and therefore decided to adopt the following as the vision of their destination:

> Gender equity means to strive for an equal society where women and men share the same rights, responsibilities and opportunities to:
>
> • pursue work which provides economic independence;
> • care for children and home;
> • participate in politics, unions and any other societal activities.[1]

The short-term and long-term goals for gender equity have both quantitative and qualitative aspects. Quantitative aspects in school work include an equitable distribution of girls and boys regarding space in the classroom and in the playground. In the long run the aim was for a balanced distribution in all areas of society, such as education, work, recreation, housework and positions of power. The qualitative aspects imply that both girls/women and boys/men need their knowledge, experiences and values to influence the development in both school and, in the long run, all spheres of society.

Some would argue that this concept is too general and requires only a minimum of change. We do not agree. We believe that this concept of gender equity, if pursued seriously, involves confronting prevailing unequal gender structures. Equity, accordingly, includes not only programmes to help girls/women catch up with boys/men. The aim should also be to promote respect for women's experiences and women's work, and to help boys claim their rights concerning, for example, caring for children and the home.

Developing a pedagogy that would contribute to the achievement of these goals was the challenge faced by the project teachers. Teachers and researchers therefore frequently discussed what the teachers did, how they did it, why they did certain things and what they should do next in relation to the concept of gender equity. The questions were related to the organiz-ation and division of groups, and to the choice of pedagogical method and content. The implication was that all school subjects should explicitly help girls and boys to become informed, critical human beings concerning the politics of gender. The teachers wanted to encourage each child to, as we say in Sweden, 'play on more strings on their lyre'. Thus they hoped to make a contribution to a change in the division of labour in society more generally.

The project group and our relations

As stated above, the project participants tried to cooperate on equal terms. Is this possible for teachers and researchers? We think the answer is yes. One of our main reasons for this view is that there is a great deal of interdepen-dence between the teachers and the researchers because of different experi-ences and knowledge. The next reason is that the nature of the project enabled a dialogue to be established between researchers and teachers. The third reason is that the project teachers were a strongly united group at the same school, and these circumstances enabled project participants to co-operate on more equal terms, despite the researchers occupying a higher status position in Swedish society than the compulsory schoolteachers.

Is it possible for teachers, researchers and pupils to come together on equal terms? It was the teachers who initiated the project and it was the teachers who wanted to change gender power relations in their classrooms. Supported by the Education Act and the National Curriculum, they acted on the assumption that their efforts were good for the pupils. However, all of us were forced to accept that, even if some of the teachers struggled to create less hierarchical relations with the pupils in the classroom, hierarchical rela-tions continued to exist between female and male adult teachers and girls and boys of school age. We were therefore prepared for, and had reason to believe that there would be, moments of resistance from pupils during the process.

Is it possible for females and males to meet on equal terms? Even if we all intended to contribute to a change in power relations between the sexes, there were moments when we realized how our actions and feelings were strongly influenced by our experiences of being indoctrinated with what it means to be a female or a male in our somewhat different white middle-class family situations in Sweden and Norway. We all had to consider that we were sometimes taking part in normalizing processes and the reconstruction of old asymmetric gender power relations in classrooms, staff rooms and the project group. We realized that we needed to remind each other to be aware of that, and each of us had to be prepared to change our own behaviour and patterns of thoughts.

Pupils' voices

As we have mentioned, feedback from the pupils – their voices in interviews and in individual written documents, together with classroom observations – was seen as having a particular impact on the development of the educational practice. It was our opinion that learning from the pupils' voices would provide many valuable insights. But what do we mean by learning from pupils' voices?

The teachers' experience is that there are differences in the girls' group as well as in the boys' group. Not all boys have power positions in the classroom and not all girls are powerless there. That means that neither a universal female voice nor a universal male voice could be heard. It is easier for some boys and girls to speak than others, and it is more likely that some voices will be listened to more favourably than others. Girls' and boys' voices represent the way they position themselves in relation to the positions they are offered by the adults and the other pupils in the classroom. According to Kenway *et al.* (1993) this way of looking at pupils and power relationships is consonant with ideas from feminist poststructuralism.

How did we handle the voices of girls and boys in the project classes? First, we decided to take them seriously, since we were convinced that girls and boys wrote down or said what they at that moment really wanted to communicate to us. However, since they spoke from different power positions, we also needed to listen carefully to their voices and to try to understand the positions from which they were speaking, in order to be able to interpret the intentions which lay behind their words. This also meant that we all had to learn as much as possible about the pupils and their relationships to each other and to the teachers in each classroom.

The voices of the adults

The teachers' voices are heard in planning papers, our common discussions – some of them taped – written minutes from telephone interviews and their report from the action research project. As well as the written report, they have documented their work in a filmstrip. Two musicals put on by the teachers and pupils have been videotaped. Our voices are heard in diaries, our common discussions (taped or in written minutes), classroom observations, written minutes from our meetings, papers and articles, and finally in this book.

Interpretation and exchange of perspectives

Each of the adults was to learn from the pupils' voices and from others' interpretations of the same data and situations. There were different and often competing ways of giving meaning to pupil's voices and to our observation notes. In this project the teachers had the most valuable and detailed know-ledge of the pupils' backgrounds and their positions in different groups of pupils in school. As mentioned above, our task was to provide an outsiders' view and to search for indications of asymmetric gender power practices and normalizing tendencies in the data.

Instead of just fighting for one's own interpretation, we decided to exchange experiences. Everyone involved had both to explain and to make her or his own interpretation clear enough for another person to follow. The next step was to try to shift perspective and learn how other people think and experience the same educational situations. These shifts functioned as a deconstructive process. By trying to carry them through, we hoped to gain a closer insight into how gender relations really appeared in the different class-rooms. One of our assumptions was that, by becoming more aware of how these relations appear during teaching situations, teachers should be better prepared to make changes in the classrooms. The final decision on how to continue teaching was always each teacher's own responsibility. Another assumption was that, by becoming more aware of how gender is constituted in different ways, all of us will be better prepared to challenge present theories and conceptions in the field of action research and equality, and perhaps also develop new and more productive concepts (see also Kalleberg 1992). Hollingsworth (1994) calls a similar inquiry approach, introduced in a graduate-level course for classroom teachers, supervisors and adminis-trators, 'teaching as research'.

Clarification of terms and meanings

During the project there were discussions about concepts and phrases that are frequently used but have unclear meanings. After much discussion the teachers came to a consensus, agreeing how these concepts were to be defined and used in the project. In addition to gender equity, which we have already defined, the most frequently discussed concepts were self-confi-dence, gender and power.

Self-confidence

During one of the first meetings all teachers used the term 'pupils' self-confidence' when they argued for their different pedagogical strategies. Even if they used different strategies in teaching and argued differently about why they were acting as they did, they were all convinced that girls' and boys' lack of self-confidence would prevent any educational efforts being success-ful. What did teachers mean by 'self-confidence'? The teachers had different interpretations. Some teachers described a person with self-confidence as one who dares to stand alone and support her or his opinion, who is aware of and will be confident of her or his abilities. Some of the participants saw this behaviour as typically masculine, and felt that always boasting about one's abilities could be a sign of a lack of self-confidence. They claimed that those who really possess self-confidence are individuals who do not always need to boast and instead leave space for other persons to act. This definition was regarded by some as typically feminine. We discussed the meanings of self-confidence in relation to contextual expectations of how women/girls and men/boys should behave, and the idealized individualistic norm of a 'normal' human being in our Western capitalist culture today. In the end the teachers came to a common understanding of what self-confidence should mean in the project and what competences were needed to achieve it. The following definition was agreed upon:

> Self-confidence is when you are sufficiently assured both to declare and to argue for your opinions, while at the same time giving space to other people and being willing to listen to their views. People who can do both can be said to be self-confident.

The teachers decided to make every effort to make boys and girls aware of situations in which – in relation to the concept of self-confidence – their present qualities would be of great importance. However, the pupils also needed to become aware that these qualities would not be enough in relation to all the challenges people meet in equal relationships. To reach the vision in their concept of gender equity, both girls and boys have to learn how to develop and use their full capacity.

Gender

If the teachers' vision was gender equity, what was their definition of gender? We had lectures about different feminist theories and the concept the teachers decided to use was strongly influenced by the American feminist Sandra Harding's (1986) theory of how power relations are structured, constructed and reconstructed. Harding argues that women and men live their lives in complex class, race and cultural relations; therefore gender appears in different cultural forms. However, highly paid positions with power and influence are held by men from the dominant ethnic group in most cultures. In the Western world they are white upper-class men. Beneath these power positions you find complicated relations of women and men from different social and cultural backgrounds. Harding distinguishes between three inter-related forms of gender: 'gender structure', 'gender symbolism' and 'individual gender'. Gender structure refers to the division of labour between the sexes; gender symbolism refers to perceived dichotomies of the two sexes; individual gender refers to individual socialization.

We discussed how the polarization of the sexes is symbolic rather than real and agreed that it must be a research issue to find out whether this applies to individual girls/women and boys/men. To gain information about the specific gender structure in Sweden, the teachers used statistics regularly published on women and men by Swedish Statistics, called 'Women and Men in Sweden: Figures and Facts'. They decided to take on the aim of challenging both gender symbolism and individual behaviour in their classrooms.

Power

The teachers also needed analytic tools to be able to illuminate different techniques for exercising power in the classrooms. They decided to utilize the Norwegian feminist Berit Ås's (1982) five ways of exercising power: invisibility, ridiculing, withholding information, double punishment, and shame and guilt.

According to Berit Ås, 'invisibility' occurs when individuals are forgotten, ignored or completely disregarded. Invisibility makes people feel down-graded, unimportant and insignificant. Unpaid work in the home is often invisible. 'Ridiculing' is when people are made fun of or laughed at for something they have done or when different labels are applied to them. 'Withholding information' means not letting people have important information: for example, about meeting times, items on the agenda and important decisions. 'Double punishment' occurs when people learn that what they do can never be right. Damned if you do, damned if you don't. 'Shame and guilt' refers, for example, to people who are blamed for not having obtained the information that is deliberately withheld from them and who are, at the same time, ridiculed for their behaviour. To develop both adults' and children's awareness of how these techniques for exercising power operate in the pupils' everyday world, the pupils were asked to perform their own dramas exploring these ways of exercising power.

Project methods

We have shown that the teachers had a vision of what they wanted to achieve, and some helpful tools. In this section we discuss project methods, i.e. what we actually did. As mentioned above, before the project the teachers' main strategy had been to use single-sex groups during about a quarter of their lessons. The first action of the project was dependent on the outcome of the question asked by the teachers about previous work: how have girls and boys experienced being in single-sex groups? We decided to ask the pupils for examples from their school work and experience. The teachers wanted a written piece from the older pupils (10–13 years old) and group interviews with the younger pupils.

Analysis of the written exercises and interviews showed that both girls and boys liked to work in single-sex groups for some of the time, and they wanted to continue this practice. However, some of the data worried us. The arguments for choosing single-sex groups were often framed in terms of negative choices. The pupils wanted to be segregated only because being taught together was worse. New questions were therefore posed. Were single-sex groups simply a period of calm where pupils and teachers could have a rest from competition between the sexes? The teachers supported single-sex groups because they thought that this practice reduced the boys' use of power. Was this in fact the case?

We decided to explore what was really happening between girls and boys in mixed-sex situations in different classes. We carried out observations in the six classrooms. In order to gain access to the pupils' experiences we constructed a class exercise with the teachers. During this exercise the pupils' task was to imagine the following situation:

> A new student of the same sex as yourself has moved into your neighbourhood and will be joining your class next week. The student wants to know what it is like in your classroom. Describe in no more than nine statements what is most typical in your classroom. If possible also try to describe in no more than nine statements what is not typical in your classroom.

Girls were also asked individually to describe, without mentioning any names, a girl they wished to emulate and a girl they didn't like very much. They were also asked to describe a boy they liked and a boy they disliked. The same questions were put to boys about boys and girls. It was felt that observations plus pupils' writings would be a good basis for interpretations and discussions of how to teach better for gender equity.

It was found that each classroom had its own characteristics, depending on the relations between the pupils and the teacher's way of teaching and interacting with the pupils. Our next set of questions focused upon the teachers themselves and how they interacted with girls and boys. It became clear that the teachers had different views of how open they should be towards the pupils in their teaching. By stressing different elements they tried to provide a balance between, on the one hand, deconstructing gender power relations without explicit intervention, and, on the other hand, raising issues involving gender power relations in the classroom and in society. With reference to the data collection, the teachers could find both advantages and disadvantages to these strategies. The benefit of not being upfront in what they were trying to do was that they avoided polarization between boys and girls. The risk run was that the message about the importance of gender equity never reached the pupils. The benefit of talking about classroom power relations as soon as they occurred was that problems could be solved at once and that the pupils learned how to be troubleshooters. The danger was that polarization could result in increased division between the students. The most important difference among the teachers was that Eva, who had initiated the project, wanted more often than the others to deconstruct gender power relations by openly talking about how current situations involving gender and power relations occurred in the classroom. Most of the teachers wanted, however, to work quietly and create situations where equal power relations, as they say, 'get inscribed in the students' bodies'. The teachers thus developed different strategies to reach moments of gender equity in their classrooms.

There was much discussion in the teacher group about which strategies were the best ones. To reach an understanding of whether and how the pupils were affected by the teaching, all teachers agreed to select a lesson to be observed, and in an interview give their reasons as to how, what and why in form, methods and content this lesson was integrated in their strategy for change towards gender equity. After the lesson we carried out group interviews with the pupils in sex-segregated groups to discover the pupils' interpretations of what we termed moments of equity (see Chapters 5, 6 and 7).

The project group had the same aim with the last data collection. To gain an understanding of what the pupils thought about gender equity at the end of the project, they were asked to write short essays titled 'A school day aiming at gender equity', ending with a description of the lesson they found most useful during that day. To gain an understanding of how they imagined themselves in the future as adults, they were asked to write short essays titled 'An ordinary weekday twenty years ahead'.

Along with developing individual teaching strategies in each classroom, the teachers presented a common framework for achieving gender equity. In this framework the teachers first discuss how the single-sex groups were to be used, followed by a presentation of what had been or should be done in relation to the three foundation stones in their concept of gender equity. To give the reader an idea of what was presented after one year of action research, we present the teachers' curriculum in Appendix 2.

Summary

In this chapter we have described how the project group organized cooperation in action research. We have also presented some analytic tools that were used and some crucial discussion points during the process. What does the preliminary guide for the researchers look like when we act as links between teachers and pupils? This is presented in the next chapter.

Note

1 In Government Bill (1993/4: 147), shared power and responsibility between the sexes in *all* areas is stressed. We wanted to define three areas of shared power and responsibility, as in Government Bill (1987/8: 105). The latter definition is also used by Swedish Statistics.

3 Action research between the modern and the postmodern

In this chapter we introduce some of the theoretical approaches that have influenced our pedagogical thinking. We start with a short sketch of the various stages through which our research projects have developed. We then discuss in more detail the theories that have served as our source of inspiration. Following this, we discuss some critical approaches to these theories, and conclude with a synthesis of our perspective.

Theoretical approaches

Towards the end of the 1980s we formulated some ideas on how to use John Dewey's theory of learning by doing, and on participatory democracy in the organization of a project in which teachers and researchers might together create changes to gendered patterns in the classroom. Gradually, we developed various methods; at the same time, we learned more about action research. Theoretically, we extended our perspectives by considering how Dewey's ideas are connected to both George H. Mead's symbolic interactionism and Peirce's pragmatism.

At the start of the 1990s, when our second research project was well under way, through taking part in various research symposiums we began to realize that our approach, regarding both methods and theory, was also strongly influenced by critiques of progress within postmodernism/poststructuralism. While not abandoning our belief in the possibility of bringing about some positive changes in gendered patterns in the classroom by action research, we became interested in poststructural feminist thinking, and especially in different conceptions of power, and came to realize that there is little room for analyses of power as discipline or suppression in the pragmatist approach. At the same time, some of our data proved easier to interpret within the theoretical frames of reference inspired by, among others, Michel Foucault and his ideas about discipline and normalization.

The concept of normalization proved productive in our attempts at analysing some of the phenomena appearing in our data, along with the concept of equity. With regard to the aim of the project, these two concepts may be looked upon as opposites when one is considering both the success and the failure of our endeavours to create more equal relationships between boys and girls in our classrooms.

In addition, in order to counteract tendencies to hierarchies in the research team, and to enhance team members' reflection, teachers and researchers learned to use a method defined as 'exchange of experience (or perspective)' (see below; see also Chapter 2).

Action research as a method for creating gender equality in school

The concept of action

Within the short history of action research, the person who most represents modern ideas of progress is Kurt Lewin. Concerning education, it is increasingly apparent that various types of positive change through action research are possible, as is clear from some of the latest works on the topic referred to below.

In order to understand fully what action research is about, it is necessary to define the concept of action. Within sociology, in the past few decades, this concept has been frequently debated. It has been used, among other things, to illuminate basic problems within the discipline, connected to the hegemony of the structural approach, in which human beings were understood as formed by society. The individual was conceived as influenced or shaped by the expectations, norms and roles connected to the various positions of which the individual became the 'inhabitant' or 'owner', e.g. positions that might be ascribed (like daughter or son) or achieved (like teacher or policeman).

In the 1970s a new discourse developed, mainly inspired by Max Weber (and also to some extent by the 'young' Karl Marx). The main idea was that for sociologists to understand human action patterns, it was of paramount importance to do research on the meanings of the actors, and to try to interpret these meanings. This new trend served to bring sociology closer to the humanities. However, it soon became apparent that the concept of action may be interpreted in quite different ways. One group of sociologists, partly inspired by Weber, but also by the English utilitarians (see Parsons 1937) and exchange theory (see Hernes 1975), understood action as rational, instrumental and strategic, and regarded the actors as always looking after their own interests. Peirce, Mead and Dewey, however, provided completely different ideas of action.

Pragmatist theory

In this section we attempt to show how action was understood within pragmatist theory. We start by commenting on the theory of Charles Peirce and then discuss the relationship between action and the theoretical approach of George H. Mead and John Dewey.

An important part of Peirce's frame of reference is that practice is primary in philosophy (Putnam 1994). Among other things, this means that the pragmatists, inspired by Peirce and his understanding of the concept of action, are considered to have overcome the Cartesian dualism:

> We cannot begin by complete doubt . . . A person may, it is true, in the course of his studies, find reason to doubt what he began by believing; but in that case he doubts because he has a positive reason for it, and not on account of the Cartesian maxim. Let us not pretend to doubt in philosophy what we do not doubt in our hearts.
>
> (Peirce, quoted in Joas 1993: 60–1)

Peirce does not aim to reduce Descartes's idea of the thinking ego; he wants to anchor cognition to real-problem situations, and Cartesianism's guiding notion of the solitary, doubting ego is supplanted by the idea of a cooperative search for truth for the purpose of coping with real problems encountered in the course of action. This also means that actions rather than consciousness are the foundations of thought. In other words, with regard to action, Peirce has introduced views about the relationship between action and research that previously had not been considered appropriate. As is discussed below, his ideas of the cooperative search for truth and of coping with real-problem situations and actions rather than consciousness seem to correspond to basic ideas in action research.

However, with regard to the issues discussed in this book, the works of George Herbert Mead and John Dewey are even more relevant. The reason may be that they are both less philosophically and more sociologically oriented than Charles Peirce, and they focus specifically on education. Mead and Dewey used as examples of actions children's experimentation, play or art. The experiment was for them the clearest and most evident case of overcoming problems through the invention of new possibilities of action (Joas 1993). Another crucial part of their theory of action is that they leave behind the idea of a society made up of isolated individuals, which was fundamental within utilitarian approaches. The same applies to the idea of people striving to attain fixed goals, i.e. furthering their own self-interests. The pragmatists' main point is collective creativity. 'The emphatic notion of democracy which Mead and Dewey used during their whole life expressed the ideal of a social order and of a culture in which the collective formation of common life processes approaches this ideal of an experienceable meaning' (Joas 1993: 250).

We now discuss briefly some aspects of Dewey's and Mead's views on scientific work (or research). What they wanted to develop was neither a specific system of propositions, nor a method that could be described univocally, but the most successful procedure for resolving specific problems of cognition. An important dimension of their approach is that the social sciences exist to aid human communities precisely in the improvement of their possibilities for collective action. In a world destitute of metaphysical certainty, they make a crucially important contribution to the solidarity of a community of human beings who collectively recognize and discuss their earthly problems and creatively solve them (Joas 1993).

Some important premises and general aspects of action research are clearly inspired by pragmatism (Ve 1992). The first premise is a basic optimism regarding people's ability to learn from joint experience in groups. Based on this joint learning, the project participants may find new ways in which to solve problems and improve situations. Another premise is that partners in interaction together must create truly democratic decision-making processes. Researchers may take part in the process as contributors of ideas and interpretations, but it is important that the researchers do not take the leading role in the project. There needs to be democratic sharing of ideas, opinions and interpretations of experience.

It may be apparent that, in some fundamental ways, action research is different from traditional science. The first point is that action research is about changing and reconstructing reality. This idea has far-reaching consequences. First, traditional conceptions of science imply that its main contribution is new knowledge gained through the *uncovering* of various aspects of reality. In action research the participants want to *change* reality or parts of reality. Another important aim is to gain new insight into various situations by investigating how changes may be put into practice and what happens during the change process. In other words, action researchers want both to change reality and to understand what happens during the change process.

In action research, the dynamic aspects of the world are underlined. This approach is different from more traditional ideas of reality, which look at it as stable or static. Kurt Lewin maintains that in order to understand a social system, one must change it – a truly revolutionary idea (Lewin 1948). This implies that any action research team needs a more or less clear notion of what ought to be changed, and what the aims of change should be. In other words, it implies that the research team interferes with reality, in opposition to the convention in traditional science that the researcher is a neutral spectator. Furthermore, Lewin's idea breaks with the traditional division between science and ethics. Consequently, ethics is also considered as a dynamic phenomenon, and the action research team may, as a result of the research process, end up with new conceptions of ethics.

With regard to the work of teachers in school, the ideas central to pragmatism – the primacy of action and collective problem-solving – seem especially relevant, in that so much of teachers' work has to do with acting in problematic situations where there is little room for considered rational action.

In our case, what we wanted was to change the relationship between girls and boys in the school situation and, consequently, as researchers we broke with the strict division between 'is' and 'ought' that is so important in traditional science (Kalleberg 1991). This means that we had opinions – based on data from various research projects – about certain dimensions in the relationships between girls and boys that we thought of as negative and in need of change. However, it is of crucial importance that the teachers and administrators (in action research the general term is 'practitioners') should share in a democratic decision-making process. Through such a process, the participants might gain new knowledge, which may form the basis of changes in action, which then must be discussed and form a part of new knowledge, a sort of never-ending process.

Mead and Dewey never directly defined their various reform activities as action research. Nevertheless, referring to the points in their views on scientific work enlarged upon above, and more particularly as we progress through the book, it should become obvious that they are an inspiration for the type of research called action research. Mead was active in the educational reform movement at the beginning of the twentieth century in Chicago. Together with Dewey, he took part in the development of an experimental school, building on pedagogical ideas on 'learning by doing'. Special for Mead was the idea that, regarding education, the child does not become social through learning, but must be social in order to learn (Vaage 1998). Considering Mead's approach to the relationship between action and science, Joas (1993: 257) concludes:

> In a civilization shaped by science and technology, the way that practical problems of all kinds are dealt with must be oriented to the level that has been reached by the creative praxis of experimentation and research by intersubjective discussion and argument in science.

As already mentioned, Mead and Dewey worked very closely together at many times, and they were good friends. Many of the points made above about Mead and his views on science also cover Dewey's perspectives. Hilary Putnam writes about Dewey: 'For Dewey, inquiry is cooperative human interaction with an environment; and both aspects, the active intervention, the active manipulation of the environment, and the cooperation with other human beings, are vital' (Putnam 1994: 171). Putnam enlarges on the concept of cooperation and argues that while for many other scientists the model is always the single scientist, for Dewey the model was the group, and the idea of intersubjectivity was crucial to him. This means that his idea of cooperation was of a certain kind: it must obey the principles of discourse ethics as this concept has been developed by Jürgen Habermas.

'Both for its full development and for its full application to human problems, science requires the democratization of inquiry' (Putnam 1994: 173).

Dewey's views on whether social scientists should include evaluations in their work are relevant for action research. Accordingly Putnam (1994: 209) writes: 'Dewey insists that to be scientific social inquiry must "grow out of actual social tensions, needs, 'troubles'",' and be related to some 'plan or policy for existential resolution of the conflicting social situation'. Hans Joas (1993: 258) underlines yet another point in this description of Dewey, and also Mead:

> With regard to politics the truly radical elements of Dewey and Mead – namely the permanent critique of the degree to which democratic ideals are realized in the existing political institutions and their impulse toward social equality which is a precondition for the improvement of institutions of true democracy.

Pragmatism, action research and modernity

An important idea basic to the approach in this chapter is that both pragmatism and action research are theories deriving from modernity. Modernity is here understood as a name for or definition of an epoch which may be interpreted in many different and internally divergent ways (Gunneriussen 1997). Nevertheless, it may be argued that one crucial idea general to most interpretations is that modernity was inspired by a belief in the ability of scientific rationality to further progress, and was a protest against tradition, which was bound by mores, religion and feelings. This epoch started after the great discoveries in the sixteenth, seventeenth and eighteenth centuries and is supposed to have lasted about 200 years, ending somewhere around the 1960s or 1970s. There is no general agreement on this. Nor is there in the humanities or the social sciences any agreement on what to call the following epoch: postmodernity, late modernity or some other name.

In Norway, action research was inspired by the work carried out at the Tavistock Institute in Britain, and started within industry as a method to enable management and workers, with the help of social scientists, to improve their relations in a way that gave room for participation, on an equal footing and within a democratic frame, of all parties (Kalleberg 1991).

In the turbulent years following the student revolution of 1968, the approach was severely criticized, and the optimism connected with the ability of the action research model to make relations in industry more equal lost much of its vitality. However, the Norwegian law on work relations (the Work Milieu Act of 2 February 1977) was seen as very progressive, and was partly inspired by this research.

The action research used within schools described in this book is clearly inspired by George H. Mead's and John Dewey's work, and especially by their optimism regarding the ability of collectivities – democratically organized – to create new and better solutions to commonly experienced problems. The work of Jean Baker Miller (1982) on empowerment, carried out at Wellesley College at the beginning of the 1980s, has been an important source of inspiration.

In a book edited by Sandra Hollingsworth (1997), the same spirit of optimism and belief in the possibility of those undertaking action research to improve situations in schools is very apparent. Interesting examples are given of how teachers, inspired by the basic understanding of teacher/pupil relationship in action research, may empower pupils in various ways. In the concluding chapter, the editor, and Susan E. Noffke, Melanie Walker and Richard Winter, elaborate on the connection between action research, education and the creation of a just and caring society. They quote the nineteenth-century US educator Susan B. Anthony, who spoke of the personal challenge of working for social justice:

> Cautious, careful people, always casting about to preserve their reputation and social standing, never can bring about a reform. Those who are really in earnest must be willing to be anything or nothing in the world's estimate, and publicly and privately in season and out, avow their sympathies with despised and persecuted ideas and their advocates, and bear the consequences.

Before we end this part of the chapter, it is necessary to refer to some important criticism that has been presented of Mead's and Dewey's world view. For example, there are very few intimations of power structures in their works, and consequently their ideas about the ability of school reforms to make lasting impacts on society are overly optimistic.

Summary

In this part of the chapter, inspired by pragmatism, we have presented a positive picture of the relationship between action research, pedagogy and modernity. In the next part, some of the ideas typical of postmodernity are presented as central to our analysis.

Critiques of empowerment in pedagogical settings

Towards the middle of the 1990s, ideas that became of increasing importance to our way of thinking were formulated by, among others, Gaby Weiner; these relate to the centrality of power relations in school. Weiner argues: 'What is often overlooked in action research as well as in emancipatory pedagogy is that institutional pedagogical relations and institutional pedagogical situations are imbued with power' (Weiner 1989, 1994: 124; see also Luke and Gore 1992). Weiner maintains that when pedagogy for empowerment is introduced into institutional classroom settings, power relations that are challenged often reappear in other forms.

In this section we discuss our experiences from the Swedish project, within a frame of reference where we look at both the possibility of empowerment in the form of greater equity between girls and boys, and the possibility of oppression in the form of normalization of this relationship.

Normalization

Many or those who criticize ideas dealing with the possibility of emancipation within feminist pedagogics are inspired by Michel Foucault's concept of power regimes. These regimes are viewed as discursive inscriptions on material bodies and the bodies' positions in different power relations in, for example, local classroom practices. However, there are disagreements on how to interpret these power regimes in relation to the 'subject' and on what 'agency' might be (see, for example, the discussion between Jones 1997, and Davies 1997).

Regarding these differences, we have been impressed by Magda Lewis (1990) and Mimi Orner (1992), who provide examples from the university level of how power rules students in relational actions. They seek to understand why not only male students, but also females, respond to teachers' gender-sensitive empowering pedagogy by trying to normalize or resist gender practices. For instance women's desire to get out of a subordinate position in a classroom was often counteracted by their fear that their actions might cause a rejection from individuals they wish to be accepted by or to have love affairs with. They might also fear that their actions could be turned against them, since the students and the university teachers can never enjoy equal positions from which to act. In these circumstances, remaining silent and passive could be the best action. According to Lewis and Orner, individuals are aware of and negotiate with these contradictory circumstances in relational actions. These negotiations often result in female students resisting teachers' so-called empowering pedagogy.

Another influential theorist is Valerie Walkerdine (1986), who argues that the concept of power and ideas of liberation in progressive pedagogy emanate from the radical bourgeoisie in modern democratic countries. She uses examples from primary schools, and argues that the positions of female primary school teachers in progressive schools are ruled by the bourgeois masters' regimes and reflect the soft benevolence of the bourgeois mother. A variety of social practices, including those in schools, are based on a concept of a norm, 'a normal individual', she argues. The labour of female teachers makes the liberation of the 'normal' child possible. However, neither girls nor black and working-class boys conform to this idealized norm. According to Walkerdine, female teachers are trapped inside a concept of 'nurturance' for the liberated normal modern bourgeois white boy. We refer to this later as the nurturance trap.

Empowerment

The concept 'empowerment' is often used in emancipatory pedagogy. Jennifer Gore (1990) points out three problems with the concept of empowerment, as it is constructed in both feminist pedagogy and critical pedagogy: (a) the presupposition of an agent of empowerment; (b) the notion of power as property; (c) the vision, or the desirable state of empowerment. However, with reference to Foucault, Gore stresses that power cannot be a property. Power is exercised in relations and exists only during actions between individuals in context-bound situated practices (see also Young 1990).

Even though there are difficulties in finding a word or concept in Swedish corresponding to the concept of empowerment, analyses of institutional power/knowledge nexus are relevant in Swedish contexts. Empowerment in Swedish schools might mean, we suggest, teachers drawing on their experiences, knowledge and power in attempts to enable pupils to seek greater gender equity. Gore (1990) states that empowerment could, following Foucault, also mean 'exercise of power in attempts (that might, or might not, be successful) to help others to exercise power' (Foucault 1980: 90).

Understanding power as exercised, rather than possessed, requires attention to how people position themselves and become positioned in relational practices in contextually unique classrooms. You can never know in advance what will come out of these exercises. According to Foucault (1983: 231) the point is that the exercise of power is not always bad, but it is always dangerous.

Frames of references: the authors' voices

Moments of normalization and moments of equity

As far as our research is concerned, we have assumed that unequal relationships regarding economic distribution and political power exist. We have also agreed on the modern vision of possibilities of greater justice and the goal of gender equity. However, we have taken into consideration the poststructural/postmodern critique of feminist grand theories and claims on how power operates at micro levels and in so-called 'emancipatory' classrooms. In other words, we realize that processes of transformation of gender equity visions into concrete emancipatory classroom contexts will inevitably be complex.

Action research for gender equity is like a balancing act. On the one hand, teachers who are too anxious to point out inequalities in conditions between the sexes can meet with a great deal of opposition. There is simultaneously a risk that teachers, in their efforts to change, themselves use the very discursive power regimes they want to deconstruct. They are imbued with them and therefore use them. Existing gender power relations can gain an even stronger foothold in the classroom. On the other hand, teachers who are too unfocused regarding their ambitions to bring about change risk maintaining the status quo. In other words, the processes of action research for change, wherever they take place, include moments of change, i.e. moments of equity as well as moments of normalization.

'Moments of equity' here refer to occasions when one is aware that gender relations exist and can be transformed. Attempts to challenge the obstacles to gender equity are, of course, the ultimate consequence. The teachers exercise power in order that girls and boys may come to see or acknowledge gender equity in the classroom. They also refer to pedagogical efforts to promote the long-term goal of gender equity. Our way of working with interpretations and exchanging perspectives (see Chapter 2) requires us to consider individuals' often competing ways of giving meaning to practices. Project participants represent different voices and different ways of giving meaning to what they regard as moments of equity. In Chapters 5, 6 and 7 we present some examples of how the teachers give meanings to teaching for gender equity and how they are able to transform this into classroom practice. We also present the pupils' reactions and their interpretations of gender equity.

'Moments of normalization', as we saw in Chapter 1, refer to explicit or implicit resistance to such attempts to redefine normal masculinity and femininity and normal gender relations in the specific context of the classroom (see, for example, Walkerdine 1986). Sandra Harding (1986) uses the concept 'gender symbolism' to describe figures of thought as to what is regarded as 'normal' in relation to the sexes. In Chapter 4 we present some examples of moments we (the authors) regard as normalizing; in other words, as we saw in Chapter 1, those moments which make the contextual and discursive boundaries between individuals visible. 'Discourse' refers to the continuous psychic and bodily interplay between people and to the choreography (Berge 1992: 177ff) defining the figures and steps the project participants accept and do not accept. During the project the teachers tried to take control of the construction of gender equity in classrooms within a context where discursive gender practices already influenced not only teachers' but also pupils' bodies and minds. Thus teachers who participated in the project tried to change classroom discourses whose creation they had themselves contributed to.

As stated in Chapter 2, all members in the project – teachers, pupils and researchers – saw themselves as inquirers, since we all contributed to the process of inquiry using our different competences and experiences. During this process one of our main tasks has been to point out any indications of normalizing tendencies, while the teachers' main responsibility has been to struggle together with the pupils to overcome normalizing tendencies and work for gender equity in classroom practices.

Epistemological questions

With regard to questions about the phenomenon of reality, we suggest that social relations and social space become real in their local contextual consequences, when people invent, make and name them. A female or a male becomes what she or he is or is not in such relations with other females and males. From this it follows that 'gender equity' and 'unequal relationships' are constructions. 'Things' are real as long as people believe in them.

However, arguing that gender equity or unequal power relations are constructions does not mean that they are unreal. We also argue that no matter how individuals give meanings to those relationships at local levels, as in classrooms, processes of power exercised in human practices, in complex ways, both control and are controlled by the real distribution of economic resources and by political power relations between individuals in the whole society and globally.

In our work we have tried to come as close as possible to an understanding of what is really happening between people in different classrooms. To be able to catch the discursive choreography defining the figures and steps teachers and pupils accept and do not accept, we look for moments of normalization and moments of equity, when teachers take actions for change in school practice. Our ambition has been to reach a more subtle understanding of the complex contextual gender discourses teachers and pupils construct, reconstruct or deconstruct and change in single classrooms, in order to be able to find a more subtle strategy for change. In this we come close to what Lisa Heldke (1989) has defined as 'provisional options', which we turn to later.

Everyone in action research, whether a researcher, teacher or pupil, is involved in relational actions, both as inquirer and inquired. We are in the world, we observe, inquire into, theorize about, and this world comes to be through our communication with it. As members of the action research project team we have endeavoured to develop discourse analysis by confrontations of different perspectives. By exchanging experiences we hoped that each of us would gain a modified and nuanced awareness of the complex gender discourse (Miller 1990; Harding 1991). We also hoped that this strategy would help us to overcome problems with status hierarchies.

When we exchanged experiences we tried to look at social relations and social space as if they were a physical space. A physical space can be described and drawn from different angles: from the top, bottom, front, back, left and right sides and so on. The best way to learn about it is to look at it from as many angles as possible, and to try to understand how it is constructed, for what purpose and how and why it is related to its surroundings.

During these confrontations with other perspectives we all tried to understand the logic in the descriptions and to pay attention to the politics of the arguments. How are these individuals related to each other? From what positions are they talking? What is regarded as 'normal' and 'abnormal'? What are the connections to the local context?

However, we have been aware of the difficulties of talking to each other on an equal basis and coming fully to 'know' the experiences and knowledge of others (Ellsworth 1989). After exchanging perspectives, each project participant made a personal evaluation of how any situation was to be interpreted and what was to be done next. Magda Lewis (1990) uses a similar approach in feminist classrooms at university level, taking advantage of struggle over meanings in transformation of pedagogy, since these moments enable greater understanding of the gendered context of the classroom, an understanding which is the precondition for creating a counter-hegemony.

Co-responsible option

This method of cooperation, with a common responsibility for the inquiry, comes close to what Lisa Heldke (1989) labels the 'co-responsible option'. She stresses the similarities between the epistemological projects of John Dewey (1929, 1958) and Evelyn Fox Keller (1985), using examples from Barbara McClintock's research. According to Heldke (1989: 104) the term 'co-responsible' evokes the communal aspect of inquiry. Inquiry is an activity carried out between individuals, who have responsibilities in relation to each other and obligations to treat each other with respect and care. 'Option' is used to emphasize the provisional nature of claims of truth, and is a rejection of those types of scientific approaches that argue that theories must ultimately be grounded in either realism or relativism:

> Rather than choosing either of these alternatives, co-responsible theorists claim that we can indeed construct provisional grounds, provisional foundations, for our knowledge. Provisional grounds are claims, beliefs, theories we take to be useful and reliable, but whose obsolescence we can always imagine.
>
> (Heldke 1989: 104)

Provisional grounds are useful 'springboards' for future investigations but they cannot, in principle, ever be regarded as 'ultimate'. Modification in the light of new evidence is part of their very nature; their usefulness derives in part from their fluidity and changeability. Heldke (1989: 111) declares the task of inquiry not as laying down answers, but as opening up new paths of discourse, and revealing new ways to deal with situations, and new kinds of connections in the world. Conclusions are always provisional, and various solutions may coexist without cancelling out the validity of each other. The co-responsible option leads to the possibility of what Heldke (1989) calls epistemological dynamic objectivities. Dynamic objectivities refer to the dynamic relationship between the inquirer and the inquired and their/our constructions of the world.

Validity

What is validity in this form of action research? Patti Lather's way of discussing validity is useful here. Lather proposes an emancipatory way of validating critical research by using what she calls catalytic validity:

> Catalytic validity represents the degree to which the research process reorients, focuses and energises participants towards knowing reality in order to transform it . . . The argument for catalytic validity lies not only within recognition of the reality-altering impact of the research process, but also in the desire to consciously channel this impact so that respondents gain self-understanding and, ultimately, self-determination through research participation.
>
> (Lather 1991: 68)

To transform subordinate positions, especially if those positions are possessed by girls or women, theoretical, methodological and praxis knowledge are made inseparable. The ultimate aim is actions in the specific context by the subordinated subjects involved (Jaggar 1983: 368).

Reflections

Our goals for action research for gender equity have been established in the context of modernity. However, we have tried not to overlook the fact, as argued by postmodern/poststructuralist feminists, that pedagogy in institutional settings is always imbued with power relations. We have realized that the processes of transformation of gender equity pedagogy in different concrete classroom contexts are complex. Working for gender equity in classrooms is a challenging task. When they are in a classroom situation, teachers cannot just stop relating to and communicating with the children. There is no space in such situations to sit apart in order to theorize. Theorizing or reflecting must come afterwards, when together with others. Our frames of reference and our methods provide data on and accounts of shared meanings within action research in order to develop new understanding of the unintended consequences of habitual or routinized behaviour in classrooms.

We have used systematized reflexivity when trying to gain a situational understanding of different classrooms in a Swedish school, and the impact on our research process, and to gain self-understanding and self-determination when working for change towards gender equity. We have utilized a research design in which we have been actively involved in the construction and validation of meaning, and which seeks counter patterns as well as similarities in the data. Teachers and researchers have used self-corrective techniques: exchanging experiences and sharing interpretations of the pupils' voices. To make it possible for pupils to develop self-understanding and, ultimately, self-determination, we used interviews and written documents. This approach should have relevance for other praxis-oriented teachers and researchers as a means of contextualizing their own practice in action.

With regard to our theoretical basis, we started out with a rather underdeveloped understanding of John Dewey's idea of learning by doing. Gradually we developed a clearer approach to pragmatism, as represented by Peirce, Dewey and Mead. In seeking to take account of postmodernist and poststructuralist perspectives on power, and realizing the danger of uncritically accepting the ideas of progress inherent in modernity, we have also applied new feminist theories and perspectives that in some important ways closely resemble our point of departure. This, we suggest, strengthens our claim for action research as a method for change in directions that we find meaningful.

4 Moments of normalization

'She is a real nuisance!' This was how a teacher described a girl who, according to the teacher, behaved badly. The examples of the girl's bad behaviour that the teacher gave appeared to be moments when the girl claimed space in the classroom. Some colleagues, who were also disturbed by girls who struggled to gain an advantage in the classroom, agreed with the teacher's opinion. Who were these teachers? Our guess is that readers will think they were male teachers. But in fact they were a female teacher and some of her female colleagues, all working to develop gender equity strategies for the project. Why did these teachers seemingly act against their own intentions, which are to give girls more space in the classroom?

This strikes at the heart of our aim of trying to create gender equality, because by their negative reactions the teachers were challenging the very work they were doing. In this chapter we analyse how these processes come to happen. The chapter is constructed around two main points of resistance, i.e. two main themes of normalizing tendencies and fear of 'disorder': resistance to superior and demanding girls and resistance to subordinate and compliant boys.

What happens when teachers try to change conventional power relations? This chapter aims at describing part of what happens, i.e. moments of normalization, which indicate how 'femininity' and 'masculinity' operate to subvert gender equity. During these moments, some project participants counteracted change and tried to adjust themselves and others to the conventional and dominant discourse of gender. No one, not even we who are committed to changing gender relations, is able to become entirely removed from the discourse. We seem to fail because we are affected by gender symbols that are already embodied. We experience fear and discomfort when actions and strategies for change appear to reach a discursive limit. This is why, we suggest, there are moments when teachers consciously or unconsciously appear to act against their own struggles for change. The two themes in this chapter, concerning 'fear of demanding girls' and 'fear of compliant boys', delimit prevailing gender discourses.

As is shown in Table 2.1, Eva, Lina and Lisbeth were junior-level class teachers teaching pupils aged from 7 to 9 in grades 1–3. Besides being responsible for the teaching in their own classes, Eva was responsible for creative activities, Lina for technology and Lisbeth for care work in all three junior-level classes participating in the project. Some of the juniors also took part in a music project with Viktor. The rest of the teachers taught pupils aged from ten to twelve years at intermediate level. Helena normally took Eva's pupils, Siv took Lina's pupils and Anders took Lisbeth's. As well as their class teachers, the pupils at intermediate level were also taught by Viktor in music lessons and Valdemar in craft lessons. Lars was a temporary teacher and, as well as teaching home economics, he shared responsibility for natural science, English and Swedish with the three class teachers at intermediate level. Further information on the teachers and the classrooms can be found in the section headed 'Classroom context', at the beginning and in the middle of each of Chapters 5, 6 and 7. See also the 'Local school context' section at the end of Chapter 1.

Fear of 'disorder'?

Resistance to superior and demanding girls

'She is a real nuisance!' Lisbeth made this remark. The nuisance was one of the girls, whom Lisbeth described as 'strong and visible' (see Chapter 7). Lisbeth was supported in particular by Lina and Siv.[1] When Lisbeth told her life story (teachers' report: 31ff) she often returned to the fact that she was an eldest child who had to take responsibility for her younger siblings. During interviews and discussions she sometimes compared the schoolboys with her helpless, irritating but charming younger brothers.[2] Although she expressed the need for boys to learn to stop their habit of seeking support from her and the girls, there were moments when she acted as a caring elderly sister towards them, and simultaneously resisted the girls' demands.[3] 'Try to do it yourself!' was a common instruction to girls in these situations. 'Don't laugh, you know how easily boys can be disturbed!' is another example of how she demanded consideration from the girls regarding boys' needs, and simultaneously restricted the girls' need to express their own feelings.[4] There were also moments when she declared dissatisfaction with girls whom she regarded as 'lazy and help-demanding' and 'egocentric when seeking praise and compliments'.[5]

Lisbeth thought some of the boys in her class were sometimes too disturbed by girls and their ways of claiming their rights. During such moments the boys regarded the girls as having superiority at school: 'If we do something to a girl, then all the others [the girls] come and interfere. But when they do something to a boy and all the boys come, then *they* say: You must not interfere!'.[6] One may wonder whether the perceived threat from strong, independent and successful females resulted in six of the ten boys in Lisbeth's classroom describing themselves as living single lives when they wrote about a day in the future.[7] Or was it some form of resistance to gender equity? Or perhaps a sign of resistance to the project?

Similarly, since, according to the teachers, a majority of the girls educated by Lisbeth become strong, independent and successful in schoolwork, one may wonder why these strong, independent and successful girls, when writing about an ordinary day twenty years ahead, expected to do much more housework than their partners. The descriptions of their lives were strange, since these girls, in other essays written on the same day, described their male classmates' competence in care work and noted how important the subject of care work is for gender equity. Since their male classmates also ranked care work as the most important subject for gender equity, and described their competence in that subject, the girls might have expected more equal sharing of home and care work from their future male partners.[8] Had Lisbeth herself, as a caring, strong and independent elder sister (see Chapter 7), become a role model for the girls and thereby influenced them to jump voluntarily into Walkerdine's maternal nurturance trap, described in Chapter 3? Could it be that Lisbeth's different behaviour towards boys and girls made the girls believe that they had no choice to act differently?

As noted in the opening paragraph of this chapter, Lina and Siv confirmed Lisbeth's view of demanding girls. Lina and Siv often agreed with each other. Siv taught Lina's former class and often referred to their similar ways of thinking and working. Lina's and Siv's classes were regarded as the calmest ones, and both girls and boys were considered to be kind and to get on well together. However, Lina's girls now and then complained about the dominating boys, and they didn't expect Lina to interfere when boys caused disruption. Lina confirmed this by saying that she did not say openly who the 'bad boys' were, and that she worked hard for – in other words cared for – those boys who needed extra help in order to settle to school work (see Chapter 6).

Over the years Lina continued to provide for the boys' needs. It is evident from the researcher's diary that Lina's questions and examples concerned boys more often than girls. Now and again, Eva accused Lina of emphasizing male importance and being too accommodating to boys' wishes.[9] In the teachers' report Lina stressed her own father's influence in encouraging her interests in 'male' activities. She also stressed the important role fathers have, especially in supporting their daughters. During observations, the researcher did not see her explicitly ignore girls' demands in order to take care of boys' needs, as Lisbeth did. Lina's classroom was calm and both boys and girls seemed to accept the order. However, while the girls did not complain during classroom observations, they expressed discomfort in interviews and written documents (see Chapter 6). While Lina did not seem to ignore girls' claims during lessons, explicit resistance to girls' needs could be seen in discussions and interviews when the girls were not present. The following utterances show Lina's reactions the first time the girls' complaints about the boys' bad behaviour were discussed:

> I think I know who these girls are. I do not take what they say seriously. These girls are in reality very interested in boys. They write exactly the opposite of what they really mean. It is not my experience that there are such differences between boys' and girls' opinions of the classroom climate. I mean that such differences have been reduced.[10]

Viktor developed music therapy lessons especially for very shy, passive and inhibited girls (Chapter 6). When those girls, after the therapy, became more visible and demanding, Lina expressed mixed feelings:

> She is a very odd person. Now she wants to become a tough girl [ironical]. She would even like to start smoking. She is impressed by Julia's elder sister, because she thinks she is so terrifically tough and looks just great. She would like to become like her. She is a very odd girl. There are a lot of things like that going on. Well, yes [a deep sigh] . . . The other girl I have talked about who never has been able to put her foot down. But now . . . now she is able to blurt out things this girl would never have said before . . . Now she finally dares to give the boys, who always fool around, a good dressing down. But how she expresses herself! [A deep sigh] Now she is able to say: You are acting like hell [whispering]. This is how she express herself now! Do you see what I mean?[11]

The boys in Lina's class also seemed to notice some changes among the girls. During a group interview they gave examples of what happened when the girls showed how they had learnt to challenge boys and their opinions. The boys provided 23 examples of when they felt the girls were not being kind to them. For example:

> Girls call out without permission.

> Sometimes they are nasty to the boys – they are teasing.

> Lisa laughs every time Rolf does something wrong.

> All the girls say that Peter is ugly and that they hate him.

> Every time I do something wrong, the girl next to me laughs.

> The girls are teasing and they freeze people out.

> They can be nasty to each other too.[12]

These might be presented as moments of equity, since the expressions are signs that some of the boys were realizing that there had been changes in the power relations between them and the girls. They could also, however, be interpreted as evidence of resistance to changes in power relations, or some boys' efforts to attack girls in order to sustain their own power positions.

Remarkably, Lina's girls also, and to a greater extent than Lisbeth's girls, seemed to expect to fall into the nurturance trap in the future. When writing essays about the future, and compared with the girls in the other project classes, they described themselves as the main caring individuals at home. If we add up all the tasks that were mentioned in their essays, Lina's girls expected to do 32 tasks at home and expected only seven to be done their partners. This may be compared with Eva's girls, who described an almost equal division of labour at home.[13] As we shall see in Chapter 6, on the same day both boys and girls in Lina's class wrote that they had learnt that boys and girls should collaborate at home and that both boys and girls could handle care work. Why, then, did the girls voluntarily jump into the nurturance trap?

Lina was surprised by these findings, since she did not regard her class as especially stereotypical regarding gender. She was also surprised because she regarded herself as a non-stereotyped role model. Lina (teachers' report: 31) commented on and explained the results with reference to the pupils' families. According to Lina, her pupils, with one exception, were brought up in what she thought of as gender-stereotyped families, with their mothers as the main carer of the home and family. Lina's explanation may be right, but one might also wonder: since the girls were obviously aware of the teacher's messages regarding care work, did they describe themselves as caring because they regarded the life of a carer as a better life? Or were they objecting to the project, or just joking? Apart from these explanations, could there have been something in the classroom that gave Lina's girls such stereotyped views of their future lives? Could it be Lisbeth's influence, who had responsibility for care work with all the juniors? Did they see Lina as catering for boys' needs, rather than viewing her as a non-stereotyped role model teaching technology? Had Lina been too covert in her message about gender equity, so that the girls did not realize that Lina's lessons were about them, their lives and their future? What was the importance of the boys' reactions and resistance?

At the intermediate level, Siv's present and Lina's former girls also expected to be the main carers at home in the future, and assumed that they would take responsibility for a much larger number of tasks than they expected from their partners. This compared badly with Anders's girls, who believed they would share equally.[14] However, as some of the girls in Siv's class expected to be single, it follows that they would have to care for the household themselves. Still, these results are surprising, and Siv's girls' essays contain, on the whole, a lot of contradictions.

For instance, Siv's girls expressed disappointment with some of their female teachers, including Siv, in interviews and written documents. They said that Siv resisted the girls' demands, while being more lenient with the boys (Chapter 6). Perhaps this is why some of the girls, in their essays, as interpreted in Chapter 6, wanted to demonstrate their knowledge of the strength of the patriarchal society and at the same time protest against it by rejecting heterosexual nuclear family lives and choosing other ways of living in a hypothetical future. On the other hand, rather than being interpreted as moments of equity, these expressions may be interpreted as normalizing tendencies, because these girls seemed to have lost their trust in equality between the sexes. When writing about the future, some girls described how their possible futures might include lives as outcasts and alcoholics, and even worse; a few of the girls wrote of a death wish. Were these girls, when writing their essays, actually experiencing fear of 'disorder' when rejecting lives in nuclear families?

As mentioned above, Siv's class was regarded as calm and easy-going by the teachers. When observing in Siv's classroom, we tried to explore whether the calmness of the climate might be explained by the fact that gender relations had become normalized according to boys' norms. It was, however, difficult to find such evidence. During our observations Siv had considerable command of her classroom, creating different systems of priority. She directed every second question to a girl in mixed-sex classes and tried to organize equal space in the classroom and in the playground. During our observations we saw no opportunities in the classroom for either boys or girls to exert power over members of the other sex.

There were, however, indications of Siv's hostility to the wishes of the girls and her greater nurturance of the boys. One example of a boy not being punished at all when doing a handstand against Siv's desk in front of the whole class was reported by girls and the boy himself during single-sex group interviews. The boys and girls seemed to have the same view of Siv's behaviour towards them.[15] Thus, there were signs of solidarity between girls and boys, which Siv experienced as to some extent disadvantageous: 'I think group solidarity can be a difficult task for a teacher, especially during pupils' adolescence, if differences of opinion occur between a teacher and the pupils' (teachers' report: 65).

However, solidarity between girls and boys was not always present. There were times when Siv's girls had problems with some boys, who were hostile to girls they regarded as feminist. The girls described expressions like 'bloody feminists' and 'whores' coming from the boys (Chapter 6). Siv was dismissive the first time the girls commented on this name calling:

> The girls' comments about boys are just a description of what these girls in this classroom dislike in common, they are not a description of how the boys in this classroom behave. Such behaviour is just what we talk

about during single-sex groups when I have relation exercises with them. We discuss what they like and dislike in boys' behaviour, for example.[16]

During discussions of 'demanding' girls' behaviour the teacher group was divided. Eva, often supported by Viktor and sometimes by Lars, referred to these girls positively, using words such as spontaneous, clever and marvellous,[17] whereas Siv, often supported by Lina and Lisbeth, often dissociated herself from the girls' behaviour. As Siv said:

> She [one of the girls] talks about justice, but this is just an excuse for being at the centre of attention herself. She wants to express: What about me then? She cannot bear being an outsider. She is emotionally unstable but strong and powerful . . . These girls have abilities to dupe people, they are time-servers. But they will be seen through later. The other girls have negative reactions to these demanding girls.[18]

According to the girls, there was no response to their complaints from Siv before they left her class.

As mentioned above, girls who were educated by Lisbeth tended to become strong, independent and successful in school work. What were the reactions to these girls when they moved to another teacher at intermediate level, in this case to Anders's classroom? According to the girls' essays, written when they were twelve or thirteen years old, they wanted equality in their relationships with men. As we shall see in Chapter 7, they also seemed to have crossed gender boundaries in the classroom. In relation to Anders's class, we occasionally felt sorry for the boys, since their interests and needs often seemed to be somewhat neglected by the teacher. The girls, on the other hand, were highly visible and audible, and took pride of place. We wrote down our discomfort in the margin of the observation notes: 'The girls are behaving just like domineering boys.' Sitting in the classroom we felt sorry for the boys, instead of acknowledging a successful crossing of gender boundaries. It was not until afterwards, when re-reading the observations from a distance, that we realized that our own reactions had been exaggerated. Notes from observations reveal that often subject content and teaching styles were adjusted and 'normalized' to fit the boys.

Anders's girls were outstanding speakers and readers in both Swedish and English, whereas the boys needed more practice in both subjects than the girls. Both Anders and Lars tried to cater for these needs. During a Swedish lesson Anders organized the pupils in small mixed-sex oral reading groups. As described in Chapter 7, the girls took on a teacher's role in these groups. Anders's way of organizing the lesson might be interpreted as him giving the girls leading positions in the classroom. However, at the same time he pushed the girls into conventional roles, since they took responsibility both for the boys' reading abilities and for maintaining peace and quiet in the reading groups. These positions for girls were meant to support and develop the boys' abilities in oral reading. In an interview, Anders rejected the suggestion that he might give the girls more challenging tasks in Swedish in relation to their knowledge: 'I cannot see any harm in pupils helping each other. I'm also doubtful about giving them different tasks in Swedish.'[19] What Anders was saying was that he could not see any harm in girls helping boys, or in using the girls to help him to meet boys' needs. Anders did not seem to realize that he was giving boys and girls different tasks during that lesson on the basis of gender.

As a teacher in Anders's classroom, Lars often used the same exercises for both boys and girls. During some single-sex lessons in Swedish, Lars left the girls to practise the same oral reading exercises as the boys, instead of giving the girls more challenging tasks in Swedish.[20] According to our observation notes, the most common patterns in Anders's class during single-sex groups were as follows. The girls were thorough in work and discussions. They read, thought the problem through from different angles, tested and documented. It seemed to be positive for them to discover new areas and to solve problems. They wanted to do the exercises several times in order to understand the results. In the boys' group the atmosphere was more bustling. The boys immediately started with trial and error methods and did not give themselves time to understand fully what happened. They jumped from task to task.[21] The following is an example from oral group work in English language.

The girls prepared oral group exercises by thinking over how to express themselves, looking in the dictionary for unfamiliar words and writing main points down on a piece of paper. Most of their subsequent group conversations were in English. In contrast, the boys started their group conversations without preparation, and the majority appeared to bluff their way through by talking Swedish as soon as they lacked the words in English. They also took short cuts by looking at the answers before they had solved the problem.[22]

Lars organized the class so that he was able to meet the boys' needs for several activities of short duration. However, since Lars used the same exercises in the girls' group, the norm for the boys' needs also became the norm for the girls. Furthermore, Lars tried to give the boys more space in Anders's class (as we shall see in Chapter 7). In English, as well as in natural science and Swedish, there were moments when the girls' wish to finish their exercises properly and in peace and quiet were opposed by Lars, who wanted them to do the same as the boys during their corresponding single-sex lesson. The following is an example of how he put the girls under stress during oral group work in English, giving them the message that they were too slow in doing the exercises:

> The girls are solving a crossword in pairs . . . One girl gives key words to the other girl. 'About a week after Christmas. What's that?' The girls

have almost solved the crossword when Lars comes over: 'Is it difficult for you? Now you'll attempt a new task and do the picture exercise.' 'Yes, but we want to continue and solve the crosswords. There is just this word left.' Lars: 'No, you have to leave this and start the picture exercises now.' The girls leave the crossword unsolved . . . Lars comes over to some other girls who also are solving a crossword: 'If you want you can leave the crossword now.' 'But we don't want to do that! We want to solve it.' They go on writing some blocks . . . Lars: 'Now all of you have to stop what you are doing in pairs. We are going to do another task as a whole group.' The girls keep on talking and writing intensely and energetically. Lars gets angry with them and shouts: 'Stop it now! We have to manage to finish some more tasks during this lesson!' . . . Lars goes on with a new exercise and all girls have to attend.[23]

The use of the same exercises for boys and girls was discussed several times by the project group. On one occasion Lars pointed out how nice and easy-going some girls' groups were and how relaxed he felt.[24] Another interpretation is that girls usually did whatever he asked them to. He also described how much more he needed to prepare before working with the boys. Lars's experiences were familiar to several other teachers and this sparked a discussion about whether one consequence might be that girls did not meet such well prepared teachers as the boys, and might not get as challenging tasks as the boys. The teachers all agreed that this was a good example of normalization, since, it seems, the girls' needs were subsumed in relation to those of the boys.

How did the boys react? They seemed quite happy with things and, when they seemed unhappy, it was not about the girls but about Anders. The boys saw him as unfair to them. They said that Anders was 'kinder to the girls' and that he operated 'reversed sexism' in the classroom. In contrast, they liked Lars. Interestingly, the boys also signalled their hostility to the project by refusing to answer the first questions put to them in an interview. It was not until they had the opportunity to comment on Anders and Lars that they became talkative. In their written work on gender equity, they made Anders invisible and highlighted the contributions of other male teachers.

As we shall see in Chapter 7, the girls appreciated that they were going beyond the 'norm' by crossing the borders of femininity. They also recognized that Anders favoured their ways of being, feeling and working. They appeared to expect to be treated equally as adults and did not seem to see living with a husband and having children as an obstacle to equity. However, they did not seem aware of the moments when the teachers pushed them into a caring role in their relationships with boys and their needs.

In Helena's class the reverse order prevailed. There were a handful of boys who were as able as Anders's girls. As described above, their former teacher

Eva was upfront about gender equity in her classroom. When meeting new teachers in a higher class these boys reacted by visibly fighting for their right of precedence over girls. The impression of a group of domineering boys was all the more forceful, since there were almost twice as many boys as girls in the classroom. The boys' ways of claiming attention worried Helena. With Lars, she struggled to educate the children in solidarity and empathy. During a discussion in the teacher team, comparisons were made with Anders's girls. But no one expected that Helena's boys should help the girls in the way that Anders's girls helped the boys, despite the fact that Helena's boys were used to take care of younger boys within what were called 'godfather activities'. This was a characteristic Swedish way of training children to care for each other (see Appendix 2). In this case it seemed to be inconceivable that the girls' needs should be the norm for what has to be done and that clever boys should cater for their needs. It seemed inconceivable in Helena's classroom but not in Anders's classroom, where girls catered for boys' needs.[25]

The boys resisted teachers' efforts to teach them solidarity and empathy most when they entered intermediate level, when they changed teachers. Helena declared that she tried hard to avoid competition, but, as we shall see, she included competitive elements in her teaching. These elements cropped up when she seemed to fear losing control of the boys. Helena dealt with these situations by seeming to go along with the boys' desire to compete. The example below is taken from a mixed-sex English lesson. The pupils were sitting in small single-sex groups in the classroom. Magnus exemplified how boys tried to take advantage of the competitive situation by making themselves the winners of the game at the expense of girls who were the true winners. He put himself at the centre of attention and simultaneously ruled and ridiculed his female teacher.

Helena announces that she is going to teach them a game called The Comb (a kind of crossword game) . . . 'This is not a competition. But whoever is ready first, cry out "Ready!"' . . . Now you help each other in groups to find English words.' The pupils do not understand what to do and the first attempt collapses . . . Helena decides to try the game again. Magnus interrupts her: 'I want to know if the others were doing bad.' Helena ignores him and writes VEGETABLES on the blackboard. The game starts again . . . 'Ready!' Magnus's group comes first. He immediately starts walking towards the blackboard: 'Now I am going to write on the blackboard! Shall I start?' The other pupils object, since they are not ready yet. Suddenly one of the boys in Magnus's group notices that they have not finished the last S. 'Well', says Helena, 'Elin's group is the winner.' Confusion. The pupils are looking at each other. But Magnus ignores everything and, giggling, he starts to write the first words on the blackboard. 'Virgin'. 'What's that?' Helena asks, and Magnus giggles when answering: 'A girl who has never been fucked.' 'It can also mean a maiden,' Helena counters. Magnus goes on writing and starts to laugh, writing, for G, 'Gay'. He looks triumphantly around. Helena asks why he laughs and asks him to translate the word into Swedish. Everyone has forgotten that Elin and her group are the winners. Magnus laughs while he cries out the Swedish word for a male homosexual. Everyone giggles and he is now at the centre of everyone's attention. Helena raises her voice: 'But gay can also mean happy!' But now Magnus has the attention of the whole room and he keeps on writing. When coming to the missing block S, he just writes 'So'. Elin's group does not protest and Magnus wins the competition.[26]

Helena's girls expressed their experiences of problems with the boys and of resistance from the boys in the classroom. Perhaps that is why the girls, in their essays about the future, took on more housework and expected less from their husbands. Perhaps the girls had learnt from reality that they cannot expect more from boys. From the evidence of their male classmates' essays about a day in the future, housework just did not seem to be on their minds. When the boys wrote later about a school day, they generally wrote very little about gender equity. Their essays were about sex-segregated groups and differences between the sexes.[27] Since the boys had learnt about gender equity from Eva and her explicit gender equity pedagogy at junior level, they should have had knowledge about gender. However, they seemed consciously to exercise power by making these issues invisible. During a group interview the boys made jokes of almost every question and gave arguments opposing the adoption of gender equity. Their comments included the following:

The boys will have all the power.

The girls will sit on the carpet and keep quiet.

Exactly!

No, we have to share, and do it every fourth night.

No, they [the girls] must never become queens.[28]

The boys' negative answers to interview questions can be interpreted as the implicit expression of knowledge about gender equity, but in a joking way. However, the boys' answers can also be interpreted as an exercise of power to ridicule Helena, the interviewer and the whole gender equity project.

These cases say something about normalizing tendencies. When we presented our analysis of these and similar situations to the teachers, we were often involved in heated discussions. In Chapter 5, Lars states that there were moments when he, as a man, was provoked by the project group and made to feel guilty by the women. During or after our discussions we often suddenly realized that our focus had been on the boys' or male teachers' needs and that we had almost forgotten girls' and female teachers' needs. Thus, although the project group was aware of how normalizing tendencies work, how boys' demands are taken care of and the need for change, there were moments when we, more or less consciously, contributed to a preservation of 'normal' gender power relations.

The only classroom that did not show these patterns was Eva's. She, more than the other teachers, wanted to be explicit about gender equity in relation to her pupils. Her main strategy was to use 'rough stuff' on the boys, while strongly supporting the girls. Other teachers thought she was too hard on the boys, and used the concept 'gender war' when describing the ethos of her classroom (see Chapter 5).

Resistance to subordinate and compliant boys

'When I was young, it was almost impossible to have a boyfriend who supported the wrong football team!' This statement, from one of the female teachers, who lived in the same district as when she was a child, illustrates the impact of sport, especially male football, on school and individual life. This small district boasts two successful and competing football teams. The teachers acknowledged that boys in particular, but also girls, who were good at sport carried a certain cachet in the school.

There was a resistance to what were seen as compliant boys and men, who did not want to compete for leading positions or domineer people around them. This resistance encouraged the continuation of competitive and domineering masculinity. As mentioned earlier, the teachers tried to defuse competition during lessons, in favour of building solidarity and empathy towards other people. Boys, for example, had sessions on care work and home economics. There were, however, tensions between the construction of masculinity arising from the impact of sport in the district and the teachers' efforts to develop more 'symbolically female' aspects of masculinity in relation to care work (see, for example, Lock and Minarik 1997). These tensions were most visible in relation to Anders's boys.

During the project Anders discussed the fact that his boys seemed increasingly to become outsiders as they grew older. He pondered on ways of supporting the boys without sacrificing his support for girls. During one of the first interviews with Anders, he revealed his fears:

> Helena's and Siv's boys are together on the schoolyard. They are keener on sport and are often together on both the football and the basketball grounds. My girls are not especially interested in sport and only half of the boys' group are playing football. I really hope my boys are not going to become outsiders.[29]

Some weeks later he remarked that his worries seemed justified:

My boys are not allowed to enter the playground any more. When my boys arrive, Helena's and Siv's boys have already created the teams . . . My boys are not allowed on to the playground despite the fact that some boys are already members of the same football team in their leisure time. Even those who are good at football have now become outsiders.[30]

At that time we read an article by the Danish feminist researcher Anne-Mette Kruse (1992). In the article Kruse describes how, with some Danish teachers, she worked with boys in single-sex groups. During these lessons they challenged the construction of masculinity in relation to sport and discussed why boys who are not interested in sport are often harassed, and why boys who are interested in and good at sport dominate not only the sporting situations but almost every situation in school. The Swedish teachers agreed that boys with high status, who were admired by both boys and girls, were often talented sportsmen. But they did not want to challenge the impact of sport.

Anders, Siv and Eva were very involved in sport and all three took part in coaching in different kinds of sport. Anders especially declared that his main leisure pursuit was coaching boys and senior teams. Experiences from sport areas made the teachers aware of inequalities regarding girls' needs and interests. But rather than changing the competitive norms in sport, they wanted to enable girls to gain equal access to sport arenas. Discussions quickly turned from negative to positive effects of sporting activities. Perhaps Anders's boys could change and become more sporty.

Lars: 'Yes, Anders's class is not a sporty class. They do not compete. Anders's pupils are different.' Helena: 'A good football player has high status.' Siv: 'A sportsman is very seldom harassed.' The teachers come to the conclusion that 'Helena's and Siv's boys have a good relationship, *because of* sport. Anders's class is different.' Eva stresses: 'Take Kristian, for example. He is clever and the driving force in the classroom. We need those boys too. He is an example of a good leader. If we are able to see his positive aspects, it will be easier to struggle with the negative ones.'[31]

At the time, there were few discussions that scrutinized and challenged the construction of masculinity in more concrete terms with the boys involved. Over a year later, and after reading his boys' complaints about him (above), Anders again made an issue of the matter:

Well, as I have said, my boys seem to have low status. And I mean, I get sad when I hear that they can say things like this in the other classes: 'How can you stand it in that [Anders's] class? They [the boys] are so . . . yes, they are so corny, and they are also so odd. If I was joining that class I would commit suicide' . . . I have talked to the girls about it today . . . and about half the group have heard comments like these from your classes . . . It is primarily the boys they attack . . . It would perhaps have been otherwise if some boys were visible and powerful, but that is not the case with my boys.[32]

With the exception of two days of single-sex camping in a course on sexuality, cohabitation and drugs (teachers' report), no serious attempt was made to help these boys to bond with the others. Why? According to the teachers, Anders's boys were taught sport separately from the other two classes; three parallel classes is one too many. They had different interests too:

'The woman culture is strong in Anders's class.' 'Yes, in all classes coming from Lisbeth.' 'At the intermediate level boys and girls do different things in leisure time, whereas Anders's boys play games *with* the girls.' Valdemar: 'When I was helping Maria's parents with some minor repairs . . . both girls and boys from Anders's class were there playing horses!' Helena laughs: 'That could never happen in my class. The boys would never do that!'

But the most common explanation was Anders's boys' 'childish behaviour':

Lars: 'It seems as if the other boys don't think Anders's boys fit in. I think Anders's boys are more immature and childish compared with the other boys.' Viktor: 'Anders's boys have low status, because they are more childish, immature, and still play with toy cars.'[33]

During these moments the teachers changed the focus of the problem from the children who avoided these boys to the boys who were avoided. Compare this with Anders's final statement, when describing the problem: 'It would perhaps have been otherwise if some boys were visible and powerful, but that's not the case with my boys.'[34] The problem was defined by the teachers as merely a question of childish behaviour caused by slow biological maturity, which they could not do very much about. So the problem did not need to be addressed. The construction of competitive domineering masculinity in relation to sport did not need to be challenged and Anders's boys' behaviour could be produced/understood as 'abnormal'.

Resistance to compliant boys often included resistance to demanding girls. One of Lisbeth's boys expressed it this way: 'My opinion is that the nature of life is that girls should be the weak ones and boys should be the strong ones.'[35] These two symbols of femininity and masculinity seemed to operate together in the discourse. Even if the gender discourse was not always expressed as clearly as it was by this boy, two perspectives might have been operating in connection with each other.

Moments of normalization with regard to competitive domineering masculinity are not restricted to boys' education. The competitive 'masculine' norm was often present in Eva's teaching, since she wanted to help girls to break boys' domination. From the very beginning her main task was to educate girls to become fit enough to fight and to become the winners in 'men's arenas'. It was therefore important for her to avoid standing out as a caring female role model herself. She left education in caring duties to other teachers, primarily to Lisbeth.

Eva had the main responsibility for creative activities with all the juniors. She often practised games and drama, to build up the girls' self-reliance by stressing abilities that make them independent enough to be able to compete on the labour market: 'I want the girls to learn how to limit their caring duties. They have to learn how to refuse firmly. To say when enough is enough.'[36] When Eva was asked to describe what qualities and attitudes she wanted to develop in her classroom, her immediate statement was:

> To dare to be yourself. To dare to be different. To dare to show others what you are good at. To dare to express your own opinions. Girls who dare to express themselves in terms of independence from men have high self-confidence. To dare to say no, to mark your limits. To avoid taking on women's roles. Pupils must dare to challenge teachers, if they have another opinion.[37]

She used among other things sport and competitive games as a means of reaching these aims: 'I have worked training the girls in football. The most difficult pedagogical hard nut to crack is to get girls really interested in boys' games and not just politely interested. To start with the boys were superior, but now the girls are catching up.[38] The godmothers [older girls] at intermediate level help me with coaching the girls and I also have a coaching parent to help me.[39] My opinion is that girls feel good when they participate in boys' strategic ball games. Now they really grab the initiative.[40]

As in the example above, she often warned the girls not to take on stereotypical caring duties and feminine attitudes. In relation to some teachers, who stressed stereotypical girlish manners, she was very critical: 'I don't really understand why they have this fashion show day at school.'[41] And in the final group interview she added with satisfaction: 'The girls nowadays never act like the caring misses they were in the first grade.'[42]

These examples illustrate moments when the contextual dominant symbols of masculinity became the norm for girls too. However, there were moments when Eva ran the risk of exaggerating the contextual symbolic male values of competition and domination, simultaneously wiping out female and male caring obligations, an equally important element in the pursuit of gender equality.

Reflections

A fear of 'disorder' parallels a fear of compliant subordinate masculinity and of demanding superior femininity. These are the dominant symbols in gender relations, and delimit the dominant gender discourse in these classrooms.

These fears create a maternal femininity and a competitive domineering masculinity, respectively. The teachers struggled to educate both boys and girls in the three goals of gender equity: sharing rights, responsibilities and opportunities within paid work, domestic work and politics. In other words, girls and boys were encouraged to develop abilities suitable for all three different areas. Neither nurture and caring nor demanding and claiming space were necessarily to be avoided *per se*. Both girls and boys needed both attributes to become equal citizens in Swedish society. What was to be avoided, however, was that women and girls took on the burden of nurturance of men and boys and not vice versa, and that only men and boys competed and claimed space for what they believed in. The project teachers did not want to create a reversal of relations, as in the example of Eva and her girls. Our interpretations from data and classroom experiences are that it was relatively easy for the teachers to work for caring, empathy and solidarity in their teaching, but much more difficult to challenge the construction of masculinity associated with sport and competition. It was easier for the teachers to work with argumentation techniques and negotiations in role plays than to take seriously the girls' challenge to the construction of femininity associated with caring.

On the one hand, these expressions of resistance and protest challenge gender equity pedagogy, but, on the other, they make visible the contextual and dominant gender discourse. These expressions of a gender discourse were created by the teachers and children in a particular context. We cannot automatically assume that they are manifested in the same way in other contexts, where other pupils and teachers act together. However, making contextual discourses visible is a necessary step for people who want, by means of pedagogical impact, to contribute to a change in the contextual discursive figures and steps that prevent gender equity. In the next three chapters we present the different ways these teachers chose to reach moments of equity.

Notes

1 Researcher's diary, March 1994.
2 Interview with Lisbeth, November 1994.
3 Observation, January 1995.
4 Observation, September 1994.
5 Interview with Lisbeth, November 1994.
6 Interview with Lisbeth's boys, January 1995.
7 Written essays, May 1995.
8 Written essays, May 1995.
9 Researcher's diary, September 1994; February 1995.
10 Personal interview with Lina, September 1994.
11 Group discussion with junior level teachers, April 1995.
12 Interview with Lina's boys, February 1995.
13 Written essays, May 1995.

14 Written essays, May 1995.
15 Interview with Siv's girls, December 1994; interview with Siv's boys, January 1995.
16 Interview with Siv, September 1994.
17 Researcher's diary, February 1995.
18 Researcher's diary, February 1995.
19 Intensive with Anders, September 1994.
20 Observations of single-sex lessons in Swedish with Lars's and Anders's pupils, October 1993.
21 Observation of single-sex lessons with Anders's pupils, December 1994; February 1995.
22 Observation of Lars's single-sex lessons with Anders's pupils, February 1995.
23 Observation of Lars's single-sex lessons with Anders's pupils, February 1995.
24 Researcher's diary, January 1995.
25 Researcher's diary, September 1994, June 1994.
26 Observation in Helena's class, April 1994.
27 Written essays, May 1995.
28 Interview with Helena's boys, February 1995.
29 Interview with Anders, September 1994.
30 Researcher's diary, September 1994.
31 Researcher's diary, September 1994.
32 Intermediate teachers' discussion, March 1995.
33 Researcher's diary, September 1994.
34 Intermediate teachers' discussion, March 1995.
35 Interview with Lisbeth's boys, January 1995.
36 Researcher's diary, March 1994.
37 Group discussion with the teacher team, January 1995.
38 Siv's written document, Summer 1993.
39 Researcher's diary, March 1994.
40 Siv's written document, May 1994.
41 Researcher's diary, September 1994.
42 Group intensive, April 1995.

5   In Eva's and Helena's classrooms: moments of equity

'The year 1919 is, of course, extremely important for gender equity in Sweden', a 12-year-old boy explains. 'That's when girls started to get power by gaining suffrage for municipal elections and the right to hold office at municipal and county levels.' Some pupils nod agreement. One girl objects: 'You're right, of course. But I think that 1939 is an even more important year for gender equity. That's when it was decided that girls cannot be sacked if they become pregnant. A job of one's own is extremely important for equal opportunity, otherwise we'll become dependent on men for money.' 'Precisely!'

This is an example of a moment of equity, heard in a debate in Helena's classroom. The pupils were discussing important years for gender equality in Sweden, and at the same time they became conscious of women's and men's conditions in Sweden. This is a good example of how teachers working with action research may change not only their own thoughts, behaviour and teaching strategies but also those of their pupils. In Chapters 5, 6 and 7 examples of similar moments are presented. These examples provide evidence of how people involved in action research can change things in their environments.

Chapters 5, 6 and 7 have the same form, and are organized differently from the previous chapters. These three chapters are structured around the teachers who worked in the six classrooms. We enter two classrooms in each chapter, one at junior level and one at intermediate level. We focus on teachers who together are responsible for a group of children (see Table 2.1), because the gender relations created during three years at junior level affect the teachers who take over the class for the three following years at intermediate level and how they are positioned and position themselves in relation to these pupils.

Each chapter consists of two parts, each part starting with a biography and a description of the classroom context written by the teacher, and going on to examine the teacher's equality strategies in the classroom and under-standing of gender equality. We also present the pupils' understanding of gender equality and their ideas on how to reach the aims of equity in school as well as in a society. Each chapter ends with reflections on how moments of equity occur in the two classrooms.

The main sections of these chapters present teachers' and pupils' equality strategies and their understanding of gender equality. They are structured around those lessons the teachers selected as good examples of teaching for gender equality. As mentioned in Chapter 2, the teachers developed differ-ent equality strategies, and in the middle of the action research process the teachers were asked to select a lesson to be observed by a researcher and, in an interview, to give their reasons for how, what and why this particular lesson may be thought to contribute to gender equity. After each lesson the researcher carried out group interviews with the pupils in single-sex groups to explore their understandings of moments of equity and how they had been affected by the teacher's efforts. This process allowed us to look back and forth across the data to determine whether there had been changes to perceptions of what equity means, and if so, what the changes were and how they took place. Further information on the teaching strategies developed for the project is presented in Appendix 2.

In this chapter we first enter Eva's and then Helena's classroom.

Eva's classroom (7–10 year age group)

Classroom context

Eva was the first teacher in this school to initiate work on gender equity pedagogy, as she became aware of boys' domination in the classroom:

> I've been a junior level teacher since 1969. In the mid-1970s I also qualified in special education. I've always worked full-time as well as being the mother of two now grown-up girls. As a child growing up I practised gymnastics and was a member of a successful team in Gothen-burg. My father, a gymnast himself, was extremely supportive and very proud of me. My mother was a nurse working with alcoholics. She was a skilled professional woman, she stressed the importance of earning my own living and she also taught me to trust my own capacities and abilities. Since the age of fifteen I've been, and still am, a gymnastics instructor. I'm a member of the board of the Swedish association for gymnasts and also a member of the international committee. My area of responsibility has among other things been gender equity. I'm also a representative in the local education committee, elected as a member from the Liberal Party. My political and social activities have of course influenced my opinions concerning equity pedagogy. I've often, when

working in politics as well as in groups connected to my interests in gymnastics, experienced typical male tactics of overlooking and ridiculing women and also of making them feel guilt and shame. In the classroom I probably appear as a typical feminist. I always try to regard my teaching and classroom practice from a gender perspective. When I started segregating girls and boys my intention was to make the girls visible. My own experience was that boys generally take over in the classroom. They speak without being asked and they disrupt the girls when they are speaking etc. In that way the girls are made more and more invisible in the classroom. During these first years my aim was to encourage the girls to claim space . . .

In recent years, my classes have had a similar structure, with a group of domineering and commanding boys. In the present class the domineering boys did not get on well together, nor did they get on with other children. In this class there was also a group of quiet boys who were overshadowed by these domineering boys. The girls have been wonderful, but in the beginning they never had a chance to be seen or heard . . . The first grade was especially laborious for both pupils and teachers. We worked hard to handle the boys.

(teachers' report: 20ff)

Eva

Eva was the only project participant (aside from the researchers) who called herself a feminist. She had had the experience of being oppressed as a woman in her political and social activities. It was very important for her to highlight in her teaching that unequal power relations between the sexes exist. When it was time for the observation in her classroom, Eva invited us to the first lesson connected to the creation of a musical, which was to be produced together by all the project classes during the semester and performed at the end of it (see Appendix 2). The teaching team wanted to make race and class issues more visible in this semester by highlighting the context around the school as primarily white and middle class. The teachers decided to illustrate the United Nations' Children Convention in the musical, and Eva and her pupils, as well as the other project classes, were to produce and perform at least one short act. Eva declared her intentions for this particular lesson:

I will introduce the musical we are going to produce together during this spring semester. The lesson will deal with similarities and differences and I will stress that every child should have equal rights and be regarded as being of equal worth. I will start with an article from a Red Cross journal, which describes girls as not being equal to boys and as not having equal rights with boys. I want the pupils to be aware of that and to consider why and if it has to be that way. After that the children will, working in pairs of two girls or two boys, look for similarities between themselves and their partner.[1]

Eva started the lesson by reading the article:

> To be a girl is no bed of roses. On the contrary, it costs. In most countries the price is hard work from early childhood. Around the world girls are born into a system of invisible work. Hard invisible work which counts for nothing. They are born into a system that discriminates, oppresses and exploits. From early childhood girls learn to support and care for their brothers. Wash their clothes and cook their food. They learn to give up food, schooling and education for the benefit of their brothers. They learn to obey their brothers. In many societies girls, daughters, are regarded as heavy drawbacks. A heavy burden for the family economy. The boys on the other hand are safe retirement annuities. Girls are also discriminated against in our country. Girls and boys are brought up and treated differently. Little girls are brought up to become sweet and kind-hearted, and to behave like 'real' girls. Boys don't have to be kind-hearted. They are often encouraged to be moderately aggressive and behave like 'real' men. Boys dominate in schools, in spite of the fact that girls work harder and gain better marks. Research has shown that boys get 75–80 per cent of teachers' time, the girls just 20–25 per cent of the time. The girls must often pay for their hobbies. Riding lessons cost a lot of money. On the other hand, ice hockey training, very popular among boys, is free. Discrimination continues in working life. The salary differences in Sweden cause Swedish girls a loss of SEK500 or more. Around the world girls very seldom get anything but hard work and sweat as payment for their work. Their duties are not regarded as paid work.[2]

During the lesson she stressed facts and discussed with the pupils ideas of how gender boundaries can be crossed and transformed. Her main message was that girls have to get rid of their dependency on men and gain access to education, paid work and the economy: 'then she avoids becoming dependent on the man. Everyone should be able to help and fend for herself.' She carried out exercises in single-sex pairs and asked the pupils to look for similarities between themselves. Eva highlighted the way that women and men, girls and boys, are treated differently across the globe, and pointed out that this does not reflect qualitative differences between individuals. She ended the lesson by asking the pupils to think about different contributions to their part of the musical, thus: 'And how can we show that girls and boys around the world are of equal value and should have equal opportunities?'.[3]

Eva's main strategies were to support the girls and to interrupt boys' domination of the classroom. As mentioned in Chapter 4, Eva coached the girls in competitive games, for example, to make them strong enough to compete with the boys at school, and later in the labour market. When we look back at data from the previous period, Eva was vocal in her opinion that the girls did not get enough support from the other teachers. Further examples of her strategies for equity pedagogy include the following, taken from the researcher's diary:

> In the staffroom the teachers are discussing leadership training for girls. Eva remonstrates: 'Girls should not learn to help teachers. They will just learn to support the bothersome boys. I want the girls to learn how to limit their caring duties. They have to learn how to refuse firmly. To say when enough is enough.' In particular, Eva is cut up about how Lars treats girls whom she teaches English. Even if the girls have better command of English than the boys, Lars uses the same activities in the two groups. Eva argues: 'Why don't you give the girls more challenging tasks?'[4]

> Single-sex groups are also on the agenda. The teachers describe the differences that occur in the different groups. Lars reports that the girls' groups at the intermediate level practically manage themselves and Viktor expresses his feelings of comfort in the girls' groups. The two male teachers comment that they do not feel as tense as they usually are when they teach all-boy groups. Some of the female teachers nod to confirm their statements. Eva raises her voice: 'It's shocking to listen to this and to realize that the girls do not get as much stimulating and challenging education as the boys get!'[5]

Eva, in discussions in the project group, took every opportunity to highlight unequal relationships between the sexes and made strong efforts to support the girls. She had the same strategy in relation to the pupils. She seldom missed a chance to provide examples of how gender could be transformed. The following is a typical situation in Eva's classroom. This was a mixed-sex classroom and the subject of the lesson was different birds and their behaviour. Eva showed a picture of a black-headed gull.

> 'The motherbird and the fatherbird help each other with the kids. Do you remember that the curlew-father had a daddy-month when the curlew-mother went away? But the father and the mother of the black-headed gulls, they help each other with the children.' A discussion on mothers' and fathers' duties in families follows.[6]

These are examples of continuity in Eva's pedagogy. There were other strategies that were changed. During the period of research Eva moderated her main strategy towards the boys. At the beginning she tended to blame the boys, at the same time giving support to the girls. According to the other teachers, she used what they call 'collective punishment' for the boys, even for those boys who were not involved in disruptive behaviour. This observation note shows how Eva reacted to boys and girls during one lesson.

During one coeducational lesson the pupils are singing, playing some instruments and taking on the roles of different farm workers. The girls take on the roles of old women and young girls and the boys old men and farm-hands. Immediately after the performance, Eva ignores all the boys and praises the girls: 'Splendid! The women were just terrific!' Later during the same lesson the pupils take part in folk dancing. The pupils sing, laugh and obviously enjoy themselves.

They twirl at the same time as they move forward in the ring. Out of the ring and in again. Clap! Clap! The children laugh as they walk with a sort of corkscrew movement into the ring again. Everyone appears relaxed. 'Sit down!' Eva suddenly interrupts, although it is not clear to the researcher in the classroom what Eva is critical of. 'I will not allow boys to keep on ruining everything!' David starts: 'But, some of the girls too . . .' But Eva interrupts: 'But the girls *never* behave like that! The girls never ruin folk dances! Now we'll try again!'[7]

Eva started to change her approach after reading the transcription of this observation. She became more conscious of the other teachers' complaints regarding her pupils. The teachers who, at that time, gave lectures in Eva's class complained about what they called a 'gender war' between the sexes that occured when Eva was absent. They also noted an increasing polarization between the sexes in Eva's classroom. This increased polarization could be explained by the boys' wish for revenge for being wrongly accused through 'the collective punishment' of all boys. The discussions focused on whether Eva could still challenge the boys' domination without using this way of punishing all boys. When being advised by the other teachers to support the boys when trying to change their behaviour, Eva sounded a note of warning, suggesting that female teachers are easily charmed by boys. However, Eva did take the comments seriously and little by little she changed her strategies in the classroom.

She decided to challenge the polarization between the sexes by creating moments when boys and girls enjoyed being together on equal terms. Folk dancing offers such moments. But she stressed that she never used 'traditional' dances which produce active boys and passive girls. Rather, she chose dances where everyone is expected to be active.[8]

She asked herself: 'How can I support the boys without detracting from the girls?' During mixed-sex classes she went on as before by trying to give girls and boys equal space, through, for example, giving every second question to a girl. In so doing, Eva pushed herself to provide everyone with questions that demanded developed answers. However, she also decided not to be so hard on the boys and instead offered support to them, especially in single-sex groups, when she worked on educating the boys to cross what she saw as the contextual gender boundaries. This is how Eva described what she did in the teachers' report:

> This project started in favour of the girls, but as time passed it became more obvious that this pedagogy strengthens not only the girls but also the boys in their efforts to become equal. Moreover, the quiet boys are given the opportunity to become visible, especially in the single-sex group ... The researchers showed that the pupils in my classroom understand a lot about equity. I have been very explicit in my pedagogy and my own teaching is of course an important factor. The pupils are familiar with my educational aims and in their written stories about everyday life in the future there are descriptions of families living in equity. But there was also a clear polarization between the sexes in my classroom ... Now I have decided to consciously strengthen both girls' and boys' self-confidence. It is of course the case that boys' aggressive actions are, in many cases, a sign of a lack of self-confidence.
>
> (teachers' report: 20ff)

Summary

According to Eva, moments of equity occurred when she tried to challenge boys' domination and support the girls. She took every chance she could to make visible unequal power relations, and argued that individuals should have equal rights and equal obligations and be regarded as of equal worth. Affected by the discussions in the project group, however, she changed her way of relating to the boys by being more supportive of them, especially in single-sex groups. She was, though, determined that support for boys never should be given at the expense of the girls.

Eva's girls

After Eva had introduced the musical (see above), the pupils were interviewed in single-sex groups. The girls appeared to have taken on board the message that people are of equal value despite individual differences. They were supportive of the school equity policy, as we can see from the following comments:

> Boys and girls are equally important.

> We are very much alike but also different from each other but still of equal worth.

> Those who have brown skin are of equal worth.

The girls expressed ideas of how gender boundaries could be crossed and transformed:

Girls should have equal rights to get education, otherwise the boy has to help the girl all the time.

Girls ought to have rights to receive equal caring duties as boys.

Don't forget to mention equal economic rights!

The girls did not just discuss rights in society. They also suggested that people have other responsibilities:

Both women and men should wash up the dishes, tidy up, do the cooking, shovel the snow away and repair the car.

Yes, you can't just get out of the house and hope to be excused from housework.

Girls shouldn't be forced to do everything.

This was how the majority of the girls expressed equality. However, two girls had different opinions:

Boys are so much better at repairing cars and cleaning the garage. They can do that.

And the girls can do things they are more able to do.

In the classroom the girls wanted to have 'The same amount of time from the teachers as the boys get.' They realized that their form teacher agreed with them:

Boys take such an amount of time.

They are time thieves.

But Eva wants us to learn how to talk back to the boys and to tell them to shut up.

Yes, the girls must interrupt strongly when boys try to take over.

The girls felt that they were able to change their situation:

Yes, we really can express ourselves now.

Earlier a lot of us were really shy and silent.

The girls had plans for their future:

Eva told us that we should first get a job, then a boyfriend and finally a child.

No, it was first a boyfriend, then a job and finally a child.[9]

This type of talk by the girls was observed throughout the project. The girls were aware of equity issues and provided many examples of boys'/men's power. They sensed the possibility of changing their situation and had great confidence in Eva. They also recognized that there had been changes in the classroom in their favour, and in their writing the girls expressed faith in a life of equity as grown-ups. At the end of junior level (when they were 9 years old) all girls, apart from three, anticipated combining paid work – in 'masculine' as well as 'feminine' areas – with shared responsibility for home and children. Compared with the girls in other classes they had a clearer understanding of the forms equal relationships need to take to realize the aim of gender equity (see Chapter 2).[10]

Eva's boys

After an observed lesson on the musical, the boys were upset: 'Just imagine! A girl can be murdered just because her family can't pay enough dowry!' When asked what they have learnt about equity, the boys echoed their understandings of men's/boys' domination and equity.

> We are all worth the same. But some lads often think they are more special.

> We are all worth the same. You can't have children without a girl.

The boys talked about rights as well as responsibilities:

> Both girls and boys have to be educated.

> Both must shovel the snow away and wash up the dishes.

> We have to learn everything the girls are good at.

They talked about all the kinds of work that both girls and boys need to experience and agreed that this includes an obligation to share duties connected to the family. In the future they wanted to be able 'to go on paternity leave. That would be super!' They did not want their future wives to remain housewives:

> Our wives will be working in paid work.

> Yes, they shouldn't become housewives.

The boys tried to show how they had changed over the years to manage to behave more fairly:

> We have perhaps grown older now, so we don't cause as much trouble as before.

> If I hit girls, they won't be kind to me.

> We have to be kind to one another.[11]

Of course, the boys did not always accord with Eva's wishes without trying to normalize the situation. Some of the above expressions may have been more or less genuinely felt. But the boys certainly learned how to give voice to their teacher's opinions and aims.

From the project data the boys' views appeared consistent. The boys certainly knew why Eva wanted them to be in single-sex groups during some lessons. For example, in the first interview the boys said:

> When the boys are together with the girls, the girls often don't want to speak up or be frank about their opinions.

> The boys are annoying.

> The boys make a mess.

In single-sex groups, the boys also experienced the classroom as less tense and charged:

> It's more calm in the classroom if the girls are not present.[12]

Early on, the boys showed that they knew what was expected of them as grown-ups, according to their teachers:

> If we get married, we have to be able to take care of the baby.

> It's good that we learn how to sew.

Whenever the boys were asked if they thought that fathers are able to take part in children's upbringing they answered yes.[13] According to our interpretations from listening to them, some boys felt that their fathers were not doing enough and really wanted them to play a greater part in their lives. When the pupils at the age of 9 (the end of grade 3) were asked to write about an ordinary weekday twenty years ahead, they described themselves as taking a more active role in housework and child caring, compared with the boys in the two parallel classes. According to their essays, Eva's boys had the greatest insights into what duties have to be done in a home during a day.[14]

Summary
Both girls and boys in Eva's classroom were aware of the hierarchy of and segregation between the sexes in school, Swedish society and across the globe. They interpreted equity as prevalent when individuals have not only equal rights but also equal responsibilities at school, at work and at home, and they argued that individuals have the same worth. To reach gender equity, the girls said they needed to challenge their subordination by getting themselves jobs. The girls were aware that they had Eva's support and that they had changed over the years and now were able to express themselves better. In the future they expected to combine paid work with shared responsibility, together with their husbands, for home and children to a greater extent than the other girls at junior level. The boys also noticed a

change in the classroom climate and noted that they had grown older and did not cause trouble any longer. Moments of equity are, according to the boys, when boys and girls are kind to each other. In the essays about the future Eva's boys, compared with the boys in the other junior level classes, had the greatest insight as to what has to be done in a household. Compared with the other boys, they were also much more prepared to share the obligations with their wives in future.

Helena's classroom (10–13 year age group)

Helena is the teacher of Eva's former class. Lars is a temporary teacher of Helena's class. Lars shares responsibility for natural science, English and Swedish with the three form teachers, Helena, Siv and Anders. In order that he might serve as a role model, Lars also has responsibility for home economics in the three classes. Helena and Lars share the same views on Eva and her way of teaching, and as they also work together when planning the teaching in Helena's classroom, they are presented together in this part of the chapter.

Classroom context

Helena: 'I am married and a mother of two boys, both at the intermediate level of compulsory school. My bachelor of education in primary education (intermediate level) is from 1976. I've worked as an intermediate level teacher since then, with some breaks for university studies and parental leave. I came to this school and this working team in 1986 . . . When my colleague Eva at junior level presented her ideas about gender equity pedagogy and suggested that we should work together to try to find new ways to realize that aim, it was natural for me to have a sympathetic attitude to her plans. Gender equity, women's and men's equality and, most of all, human beings' equal worth have always been my principles. I have never experienced any restrictions myself. In relation to my parents, everything was allowed. My sister and I were always supported by our parents and they believed in possibilities for us. It was taken for granted that we should have a good education, so that we would be able to get along well and stand on our own feet. Outside my own family I have of course experienced inequality and, even though Sweden is regarded as taking the lead in this area, I have realized that work for gender equity must continue. We have not reached our destination yet.

(teachers' report: 68ff)

Lars: I am 48 years old, married with three children: two girls aged 22 and 18 and a boy of 14. I became an intermediate-level teacher at the

end of the 1960s and have since then primarily worked at the intermediate level. I've worked in this team since 1981, except for some
years of work abroad and at a special recreational centre and a day
school for children with behavioural problems. When our colleague
Eva initiated this gender equity project it was a matter of course for me
to join the group. The ideas seemed reasonable and, besides, equity has
always been self-evident to me . . . Unfortunately this project was carried out at the same time as the implementation of the new national curriculum. These circumstances have therefore meant periods of almost
unreasonable burdens of work . . . Before we started the project I
thought I was relatively aware of the question of gender, especially since
I, a man born in the 1940s (with all that this implies), have been living
with a feminist for 23 years . . . It is a delicate and above all difficult
task, especially for us men/boys, to make visible complicated gender
relations. We often, or we think we often, get pushed into the prisoner's
dock. Not infrequently we are also provoked. We can understand this
in a theoretical and intellectual way, but in reality it is hard emotionally.
The task becomes even more difficult in a classroom with children
between the ages of ten and thirteen. You always run the risk of becoming too eager and of pestering the children with too much lecturing and
adult argument. My opinion is that we must try to create situations that
encourage understanding of and sympathy with gender questions
instead of burdening our pupils with guilt. I think it is better to 'live
equal relationships' than just to talk about them. We all know that it is
easier for a child to imitate adults' behaviour than to follow their
instructions, in the same way that a brilliant week of interdisciplinary
work on democracy may become totally worthless if you don't in practice live up to the principles of democracy. If a teacher moves too
quickly and highlights the equality issues inherent in children's behaviour before the children are capable of understanding abstract notions,
then we run the risk of confirming and possibly increasing the polarization between girls and boys. We run the risk of failing to respect the
pupils, when theorizing their own behaviour and therefore demonstrating the unequal power relations which we take such pains to avoid.

(teachers' report: 76ff)

When Helena took over Eva's class, Eva had not shifted in her pedagogy.
This class had not experienced Eva's new ways of supporting boys' gender
boundary crossing. Her main strategy was for this class to strengthen and
support the girls, combined with being harder on the boys. This is how
Helena described this class in the teachers' report:

There were fourteen boys and eight girls in my intermediate level group.
A lot of them had known each other since they were small children.
When the school started at junior level these children were brought

together, some from a pre-school group, some from different full-time pre-school centres, and some from different child-minders. Many of the boys were active in football and indoor bandy (a Swedish game). Several boys were also interested in fishing and soon music became a big interest. There tended to be few firm relationships. Instead, they saw each other in different constellations during leisure time. Most of the girls were very interested in animals. There were a lot of pets in their families and a couple of them were occupied with riding. Sports, stamp collection and participation in different associations were other leisure hobbies for the children. At the age of ten and at the beginning of grade 4, the girls viewed each other mainly in terms of firm best friends relations. However, one of these relations was a trio and one of these girls often felt left out at school . . .

Creativity, spontaneity, strength and sense of humour were positive characteristics of these children and of course that had to be encouraged and supported. Ideas from this group developed into projects for the whole school; for example, the collection of clothes for Russian people and the purchase of pieces of rainforest. But the class also had its drawbacks. There were few common interests among the pupils. Instead they tried to control each other and very quickly showed up others' mistakes or omissions. They were quick to focus upon others' negative sides instead of the positive ones. It was easier for them to notice obstacles instead of possibilities. There were no differences between boys and girls in this matter. Some boys also had the habit of commenting negatively on other pupils' points of view, or with their body language expressed their negative opinions of other pupils. Some of these boys were, with good or bad points, very competitive. All this had, of course, an influence on the atmosphere in the classroom. The outcome was that some boys and the majority of the girls felt it hard to express themselves in the classroom.

(teachers' report: 68ff)

As well as being taught by Lars, this class was taught by Viktor for music and choir singing and Valdemar for woodwork and metalwork. Although coming from different angles, the teachers had similar criticisms of the individualistic and competitive climate of Eva's classes.

Lars: There are many clever boys in the class . . . I have good contact with the pupils in Anders's and Siv's classes, but I have difficulties and cannot be quite myself in Helena's class . . . The group is very heterogenous in all respects, regarding knowledge as well as confidence. Eva has worked too little with relationship exercises but Helena has been working hard with that since grade four . . . In Helena's class they make comments about each other all the time. They are insecure and they change their minds as soon as they find out that their pals believe something else. They are simply afraid of making fools of themselves. This is especially striking in the girls' group.[15]

Viktor: The boys are not as good in music as the girls are. Education in music is preferred by girls. The boys lack good role models, especially in choir-singing. There are problems in particular with one boy in Helena's class. This boy is the best in music, but he thinks he always has the right to go first.[16]

Valdemar: In woodwork and metalwork one has to have strong will and patience. You can't compete and be in a hurry, so Helena's boys have difficulties in being able to behave according to these norms.[17]

The girls were not mentioned as having these problems in woodwork and metalwork.

Helena and Lars

Helena and Lars were critical of Eva's way of using what they call 'collective punishment' of boys. In their opinion punishment cannot create equity. 'Eva's pedagogy just sweeps the problems under the carpet and these problems emerge during other teachers' lessons.'[18] To start with, Helena and Lars wanted to relate to the boys in other ways. As Lars expresses above, moments of equity come when one can 'create situations that encourage understanding of and sympathy with gender questions instead of burdening our pupils with guilt'. Helena and Lars agreed that gender equity requires good relationships between the sexes, and stressed this in relationship exercises.

Helena had been teaching Eva's former pupils for two and a half years when the observation took place. As she explained:

Since the children of today are watching TV and are going to the cinema a lot I ask the pupils to think of a person in a film, a person who has affected them in some way. I ask them to write down the names of some of these film stars. Afterwards I get the group together in a circle so that each of them can present and discuss which qualities affect them. I assume that girls and boys will choose different qualities, so I use single-sex groups. I want everyone to reflect on what and why things affect them. I follow up the discussion using a gender perspective by asking: Who do the pupils select? Which qualities are attractive? I also discuss stereotypical female and male behaviour in relation to their answers. Both boys and girls need to discuss and reflect upon those issues with people with the same sex.[19]

During the two lessons the pupils talked to each other about their selections and the qualities they admire. All the boys and most of the girls selected boys and men. Helena encouraged them to enlarge upon their choices and to be more specific. She also asked questions like: 'Would you like a friend like this? Would you like him to be your dad?'.[20] However, she did not discuss their answers in relation to stereotypical gender patterns, despite her declaring that she would in the interview before the lesson.

During the project Helena tried to be careful not to lecture too much on gender issues. When the pupils' individual written essays during grade 5 revealed the girls' dissatisfaction with the habit of negative comments in the classroom, and when classroom observations carried out at the same time revealed boys' dominance[21] (written essays and observations, spring 1994), Helena developed more positive strategies for achieving gender equity:

> I want to build on the pupils' positive sides. I want them to learn how to show consideration, tolerance and respect. To show respect has several meanings: to meet individuals, to thrash things out, to show respect. To accept a rush of emotions, but with some restrictions. One's own behaviour must never become oppressive to other people. I want to keep on with the activities in single-sex groups with, for example, discussions about relationships in literature. We use these discussions to deal with anger, tears and puberty.[22]

Helena described (teachers' report: 69ff) practical work carried out in relation to these aims. To create a more appreciative milieu, Helena developed different 'appreciation exercises'. For example:

> I start in single-sex groups and the task is to find out what they appreciate about their classmates. They write down something positive about everyone in the group on a piece of paper. One is always able to say something positive, but what is said depends on how much you know the person in question. The important thing, though, is to be honest. We cannot run the risk that the receiver regards the message as false. Every child gets a yellow sun and every appreciating message is written down on a sunbeam and expressed loudly to the group . . . In this class there were requests in both groups to write about the rest of the class, the girls about the boys and vice versa. So we did, and every child gained one more yellow sun with sunbeams and the two suns were taped up inside the desklid to spread warmth to every child.
>
> (teachers' report: 74)

Helena developed her pedagogy as: 'one way of teaching the pupils how to show consideration, tolerance and respect is to learn to know each other better.' She therefore used the single-sex groups for conversations on different subjects in a round. In the boys' group her strategy was to defuse competition, while stressing the possibility of everyone performing well:

> In the boys' group it was important to win and to be the best. We talked about that from different angles. I felt it was important to avoid

activities that very easily become competitive and instead find exercises that strengthen cooperation. If one wins another loses. Only one person can be the winner but everyone can do well.

(teachers' report: 74)

In the girls' group she encouraged the girls to stand up for their own opinions despite possible disagreements:

In the girls' group the emphasis is more on learning how to be able to make a distinction between person and thing, and daring to stand up for a situation or an opinion despite running the risk of 'her getting angry if I have other opinions'. We talk about the fact that we all are different, with different thoughts, and that nobody really wants to have a friend who always agrees.

(teachers' report: 74)

Helena also addressed how to relate to persons who try to assume power and reported an occasion when this knowledge was used by one of the girls against Lars:

During these exercises I used Berit Ås's examples of five ways of exercising power [see Chapter 2]. Sometime after that, Lars was told by a girl, when he was fixing his watch as she was speaking: 'Now you show that you don't listen to me! You make me invisible.'

(teachers' report: 71)

To help the pupils to find solutions to different problems Helena used what she called 'value exercises'.

We find out about our own values, express our attitudes in the matter and listen and learn from each other's values . . . We saw a film based on William Golding's *The Lord of the Flies*. Next day we worked with value exercises and discussions in single-sex groups . . . One question was: 'Whose fault was it?' The majority of both girls and boys identified the separatist leader Jack as the scapegoat. But some girls and boys considered that everyone was to blame. Their argument was that if the masses had not followed Jack, this evil would not have happened. We had a general discussion about the responsibilities of the quiet masses, everybody's responsibilities and the fact that passivity makes us support what we in reality would like to dissociate ourselves from.

(teachers' report: 72–3)

Lars claimed that his ambitions were in line with Helena's: 'You cannot teach children anything if they don't have confidence in themselves and in the group. The first thing one has to invest in is the classroom climate and good relationships between the children.'[23] But, in contrast to Helena, Lars talked more about the importance of the teacher as a leader:

Children follow the herd. Therefore they need a firm leader. It's important that the teacher makes the rules visible. Children have to learn to
work together. To be able to do that they need supervisors. Individualism can be accepted, but not at another person's expense. I make things
visible by saying, for example: 'How does Kalle feel when you do these
things?' More and more pupils think they have rights of precedence and
they are not happy with it. The teacher has to know all the ropes and
not let these things go. Parents have difficulty in setting limits for their
children. The teachers and the collective are important ... I have
changed during these years. Gender questions are more visible to me
now than before.[24]

Lars also avoided too much lecturing on gender questions. However, as
we saw above, Lars confessed that this is a difficult task: 'It is a delicate and
above all difficult task, especially for us men/boys, to make visible complicated gender relations.' Helena avoided making explicit complicated gender
relations, but she confessed that she was not sure whether she was on the
right path or not. She was sometimes disappointed about how things turned
out between girls and boys in her classroom. Her views at the end of the project remained tentative.

I still don't know how. Things one has to be explicit about; that is, all
humans' equal worth and such things. This is self-evident. As a parent,
of course I have to make explicit what I think ... I still think that parents should express their fundamental values. It is quite natural for me
to do so. But if I make a comparison with my pupils, then my opinion
is ... well I don't know if I always explicitly ... But there are things I
sometimes do at home too, without making it explicit to the family, but
of course I would bring up for discussions things like this [gender
issues].[25]

When the project had ended she was satisfied with what she had done so far
but conscious that she had to go further.

Summary
As we have seen, Helena and Lars did not call themselves feminists. They
both took part in the project because human beings' equal worth was a self-
evident principle for them. Helena and Lars were both critical of Eva's strategies for reaching gender equity, which they regarded as harsh, simplistic
and providing a bad competitive climate in the classroom. In particular, they
were critical of Eva's tendency to blame the boys for everything. According
to Helena and Lars, the best way to reach moments of equity is to live out
gender equity in actions, and to stress pupils' positive sides. As we have seen,
to encourage this Helena used appreciation exercises in her classroom, and
to counteract competition she used relation exercises. In the boys' group she

stressed the possibility of everyone performing well and the lack of need for a winner, and in the girls' group she encouraged the girls to stand up for their opinions in the face of criticism. However, occasionally Helena was hesitant and disappointed with the normalizing tendencies in her classroom, and Lars admitted that men/boys had more difficulties with making visible complicated gender relations.

Helena's girls

Immediately after the observed lesson involving the selection of film stars the girls were asked what message they thought Helena wanted to give them. They looked at each other and were quiet. After a while they said that Helena was often in the habit of chatting with them in a circle. But they did not really know why she did this. No one could remember her telling them. The girls guessed:

She wants us to express our opinions.

She perhaps wants to know what we think about movies.

No, I think she is up to something special.

When asked about single-sex groups, they continued:

I talk much more in the girls' group than in coed classes.

But if that was a case of equity, we should have talked more about equity, shouldn't we?

And this was just our memories and nothing more to learn.

They returned to the fact that they were in a single-sex group. 'I think she does this because we'll have the opportunity to be alone . . . They [the boys] perhaps laugh if we say things wrong or something like that?' But they again stressed: 'This can't have anything to do with equity.' They referred again to the films:

Perhaps she wants to see if boys and girls like different kinds of films.

Yes, different tastes in films.

Yes, the boys perhaps choose the hardest war films.

The boys still think it is cool with things like: Hit him on the jaw!

When asked what equity between girls and boys in the classroom meant, they first answered that the equity project only took place when they were divided into single-sex groups. When asked about their own understandings, they looked surprised and bewildered: 'I don't understand this! It *is* equity in the classroom, when we are together!' When asked to be more specific they discussed back and forth, and finally:

This is what the whole project is about – to deliberately choose activities usually associated with boys in school.

It should not matter if it is a girl or a boy who does things.

Now I dare to speak up more often. But of course it is easier in a girls' group.

To stand up for our opinions.

We should dare to answer, even if we are not sure that the answer is right.

Well, I'm not particularly afraid of talking in front of the boys.

The girls also noticed a reduction in boys' domination of the classroom and in classroom climate:

Earlier they could sit and make faces and say ironically: 'You, you are really smart!'

They used to do things like that, but not any more.

Just Peter.

And I don't care any longer if they tease me. It makes no difference.

Now Helena directly sets to work at the boys too, so it's better now.

When asked about what gender equity would mean when they became adults, most of the girls talked about doing the same amount of work as their husbands:

My opinion is that both have to cook, both have to wash, both have to wash the dishes.

Both must take care of the children.

A few, however, had objections:

If one of them is better at doing something and doesn't want to learn this and the other perhaps is better at other things.

Yes, they should do what they are most interested in and clever at. My father is better than my mother at cleaning and tidying up. My mother is more strict about washing up the dishes and more careful with the dishwasher.

The girls' opinions concerning paid work followed the same pattern. Most of them believed that sex has nothing to do with what profession you should have:

It should not matter what you do.

And it should be equal, that about equal salaries.

As well as washing . . . like working in an office – everyone can do that.

Yes, and daddies can work as child-minders.

The girls were not sure about Helena's opinion regarding equity in paid work. However, they thought that she believed that men and women should work an equal amount of unpaid work as well as an equal amount of paid work.[26]

At the end of the last semester, when the pupils wrote about 'a day in school and signs of equity' and described which lesson they found most useful (see Chapter 2), all the girls in Helena's class mentioned the value of single-sex groups. Most important were the lessons in English and sport, followed by Swedish and work done in connection with the musical about the United Nations children's convention. When they differed it was not related to the subject content. The key point was that they dared to do more things and performed better in single-sex groups.

In their short essays about an ordinary day twenty years hence the picture drawn was utopian. For example, all the girls lived a life with a husband and children. They combined paid work with caring for home and family, and they expected their husbands to do housework. They were in different and not particularly female-oriented paid work: for example, doctor, researcher, interior designer. One of them described herself as the breadwinner and her husband as unemployed.[27]

Helena's boys

Immediately after the 'movie lesson', the boys were asked what message they thought Helena wanted to give them. They started to discuss memories:

This is because we will remember.

Yes, and then she [Helena] steals the memory.

They were reminded of the fact that they were still in a boys' group. 'Oh, this is about gender equity or something!' When asked about what equity means, one said: 'I don't know.' The rest were silent. They were asked again: 'What does your teacher want to say?' The silence remained until a boy hit another with a ruler at the same time that one boy said: 'She [Helena] probably thought that Sweden should become more independent.'

They never gave direct answers to the questions about gender equity. Their answers and discussion suggested that the boys preferred to explain their knowledge of what males' and boys' domination implies and what the gender equity project is about through jokes. Let us look at a part of the interview where they discussed Helena's ambitions regarding gender equity:

I think that Helena's opinion is that the girls have to assert themselves
. . . if both boys and girls throw snowballs, then it's just the boys who
have to own up.

Exactly. That is her [Helena's] theory about school.

No, she is in fact quite impartial.

I think it is quite fair in the classroom.

When asked to be more explicit about fairness in the classroom, the boys
started to complain about the difficult questions as impossible to answer.
When asked about adults and gender equity, they offered the following
answers:

I think the mummy should wash up the dishes and do things like that
and the daddy should switch on the TV and make a fuss if anyone does
something foolish.

No, I think both of them should have it equally good.

And the father should do the washing up and ironing.

And the mother should work and earn money.

And the father, he must earn less money.

I think that the mother should have the right to become Father Christmas.

Yes, otherwise it is sex discrimination.[28]

When we look back at the data, the boys seemed to feel confident with
themselves and school at intermediate level. They had no complaints when,
in grade 5 at the age of 11, they were asked for their opinions of education
in sex-segregated groups. They liked to be together with other boys, they
argued, because they had common interests, it was easier to work, there
were less babble, less nagging and more discussions.[29] When they described
their classroom climate they had a few complaints about the food and cleaning in school but were mostly positive. The most positive statements dealt
with good and decent friends, good and decent teachers, enjoying school
and being clever and bright.[30]

The boys were also asked to write about a day reflecting gender equity
and, just like the girls, they wrote only about single-sex groups. When they
were asked to rank subjects most useful to gender equity, the picture was
very diverse and split. In the same essays home economics was ranked highest by three boys and Swedish by two boys; the other seven boys chose
different subjects. Most comments concerned similarities in the boys' group
and differences between boys and girls.

Perhaps that is why they chose rather typical masculine paid work in their
essays about the future. The most popular choice was to become an ice

hockey professional. Four boys described themselves as such. The others were working as, for example, fighter pilot, sailor, policeman, mechanic. They all presented themselves as living in a relationship with a woman, but four of them would have no children. They did not mention housework much in their essays. These twelve boys described five tasks dealing with taking care of children and dogs. On the other hand, they did not describe themselves as receiving daily housekeeping service from a woman. Compared with the other boys in the other classes, they described the largest range of leisure activities. Half of the group thought they would watch TV and the rest would enjoy themselves with their partners, going out with friends, fishing and playing music.[31]

Summary
The pupils brought the legacy of their relations with Eva into Helena's classroom, where they met Helena's and Lars's alternative way of relating to them. Neither the girls nor the boys could make any immediate connections to gender equity issues they were confronted with in the observed lesson. They were insecure about Helena's standpoint regarding gender. They were, however, able to recognize the single-sex groups as evidence of the gender equity project in the school. When talking about gender issues, both girls and boys showed in different ways that they had considerable knowledge of gender equity. The girls noticed changes in their relations with the boys over the years and argued that there had been a decrease of boys' dominance. They appreciated the way in which Helena dealt with the boys. The girls also noticed their own increased self-confidence and believed that a gender equity climate had been created in the classroom, particularly because they were not afraid to stand up for their own opinions. In this classroom, with almost twice as many boys as girls, single-sex groups were seen as of utmost importance.

The girls argued that sex should not affect paid or unpaid work in any way, and in the future they expected to be in a variety of jobs. The boys related to the researcher by making jokes, but their answers showed that they knew what was expected of them in terms of gender equity. However, their responses also indicated that they needed to be seen not to care about gender. For them, single-sex groups were preferable to mixed-sex groups, because they were able to do things in 'their way' and to develop their interests without being disturbed by the girls. They also discussed their intention, as adults, of working in male-associated jobs. However, they did not expect to rely on their girlfriends to do the housework, and in fact went as far as including them in their own proposed leisure activities.

Reflections

This innovative project in Sweden was started by Eva because of her great passion for gender equity. Since she was also a member of the Swedish

Liberal Party, she saw the positive effects of individualism, independence and competition. It might be argued that Eva overstressed these effects. Although she sometimes discussed parental obligations to caring for children and home, she tended to leave the main responsibility for care work to Lisbeth. Eva's pedagogy, being explicit about the aims of gender equity, appeared to be working in that the pupils learnt about equity at a rhetorical level. In their interviews both girls and boys gave examples of this. The girls also felt supported by Eva and pointed out that they had learnt to claim space in the classroom.

However, the pupils' responses might be seen in another way. It could be argued that they had merely learnt their lessons well, without developing a deeper understanding of why girls and boys should be equal. The boys, in particular, showed by their actions that they did not appear to have gender equality at heart. For the boys, Eva's pedagogy could be seen as working only on a superficial level. It might be argued that Eva's way of supporting girls and simultaneously picking on boys increased the polarization and hostility between the girls and boys in the classroom. The teachers of Eva's pupils highlighted the negative effects of Eva's approach, and she was asked to think again about her behaviour towards the boys. After this, Eva attempted to eliminate the polarization between girls and boys by using activities which girls and boys might like to perform together, such as folk-dancing. However, she did not have enough time to see the results of this change before the pupils reached the age of 10 and left Eva's classroom and the junior level for the next level.

Eva on the one hand and Helena and Lars on the other were often apparently on a collision course during the project when politically or pedagogically arguing for how to achieve equity in classrooms as well as in society. Helena and Lars argued that Eva's approach tended to sweep the problems under the carpet. Helena and Lars preferred to identify problems and to gain a deeper understanding of how the hostility between girls and boys could be reduced. To understand the pupils better, they adopted single-sex groups for discussions. They also used single-sex groups to lessen individualism and competition among the pupils, while at the same time stressing solidarity and understanding. Instead of always highlighting gender issues, as was Eva's strategy, they attempted to promote solidarity and understanding through different actions: for example, through value and appreciation exercises. Through this their pedagogy seemed to become deeper and more developed. Moreover, they seemed to have been successful in their efforts to create confidence among pupils and teachers. The girls expressed the view that the classroom climate was less hostile than before, and that there was in fact greater gender equity. Both boys and girls seemed to have confidence in their teachers, and an appreciation of the single-sex lessons.

However, Helena and Lars did not challenge the male norm in the classroom. Thus, during the observed lesson both girls and boys chose men as their preferred role models, and Helena did not, as she intended, follow up the discussion using a gender perspective. In their interviews the girls argued that gender equality means that they are able to behave more like boys.

It also seems that it was easier to be a male teacher in this classroom. Lars expressed more faith in the possibility of setting strong boundaries for pupils' hostile behaviour. Another problem was that the boys withdrew from the discomfort of being with girls by establishing separate spaces of their own. They created a distance from the girls and girls' activities at school, as well as in a perceived future life as adults. Helena and Lars were aware of these tendencies but could do little, as at age 12 the pupils would soon be leaving them for teachers at more senior levels.

Notes

1 Interview with Eva, December 1994.
2 The article is published in a Red Cross Journal: *Barnen och Vi*, no. 5, 1990.
3 Observation, January 1995.
4 Researcher's diary, September 1994.
5 Researcher's diary, January 1995.
6 Observation, May 1993.
7 Observation, May 1993.
8 Researcher's diary, September 1994.
9 Interview with Eva's girls, January 1995.
10 Written essays by Eva's girls, May 1995.
11 Interview with Eva's boys, January 1995.
12 Interview with Eva's boys, autumn 1993.
13 For example observation, September 1993.
14 Written essays by Eva's boys, May 1995.
15 Interview with Lars, November 1994.
16 Interview with Viktor, October 1994.
17 Interview with Valdemar, October 1994.
18 Group discussion, June 1994.
19 Interview with Helena, February 1995.
20 Observations in Helena's classroom, February 1995.
21 Written essays and observations, spring 1994.
22 Interview with Helena, September 1994.
23 Interview with Lars, November 1994.
24 Group discussion with the whole teacher team, February 1995.
25 Taped group discussion, March 1995.
26 Interview with Helena's girls, February 1995.
27 Written essays, May 1995.
28 Interview with Helena's boys, February 1995.
29 Written essays, autumn 1993.
30 Written essays, spring 1994.
31 Written essays, May 1995.

6 In Lina's and Siv's classrooms: moments of equity

In this chapter we first enter Lina's junior-level classroom and then move on to Siv's intermediate-level classroom. Viktor, the music teacher, is also important to the project, as he gets involved in efforts to strengthen the shy, quiet, and inhibited younger girls. Some of Lina's girls joined a form of music therapy class with a drum programme especially adapted for them. Viktor and Lina are therefore presented here together. Viktor and Valdemar are presented together with Siv in the second part of this chapter, since they both contributed to lessons in her classroom. It might seem that the same data appear repeatedly in different parts of this chapter. However, we feel it is worth including these data, since we believe it is important to report on what different teachers and pupils say about gender.

Lina's classroom (7–10 year age group)

Classroom context

Lina: I'm a junior level teacher. My teacher's certificate is dated 1966. In the first years after graduation I stayed at home with my daughter, and I gave birth to my son in 1969. Since my own mother was employed part-time and did her work at home, she was able to help me with child-minding at relatively short notice. This made it possible for me to take short-term temporary posts.[1] In 1973 I got a post with conditional tenure in this school, where I still work. Since I always have liked work-ing with children and young people and since I have always found it important in my profession to pay attention to every single child's needs, it did not at first seem very important to me when my colleague Eva in the parallel classroom asked me to join a project working with gender equity pedagogy at our school. But at the same time I had an intuition of a dimension that I was not so aware of and had not reflected much on, namely girls' and boys' different needs. In particular, how could support be given to the quiet girls? Should the boys who take up a lot of space in the classroom and demand too much of my time be treated in a different way? What usually happens to the quiet boys? The more I reflected on these questions the more I realized that I had, in a more conscious way, to take the concept of gender equity seriously in my teaching . . .

I had responsibility for all pupils' education in technology at the junior level. This has been a very practical arrangement since all material could be placed in the same classroom . . . Why did I choose to take responsibility for technology? I'm not really a professional, but of course I've had in-service training in science and technology. I remember very clearly when I participated in a mixed-gender in-service group and our task was to do some laboratory work in the field of electricity. Before the women had even read the laboratory description through, the men had already solved the task and had started on the next one. The same thing happens at the upper level of compulsory school! I therefore chose to teach technology at junior level and to use sex-segregated groups for that purpose. Why technology? My father wanted a son but he got a daughter! No more children were born. What does a father do, when he loves his daughter? He lets her take part in things a son would have taken part in. I was initiated early into the secrets of changing fuses, how a motor works, car driving at an early age – to my mother's consternation etc. The strength a supporting father gives to his daughter, she bears through her whole life.

(teachers' report: 25)

Viktor: I am 44 years old, I'm married and have two sons. During my childhood years my parents worked full-time, which meant that my brother, two sisters and myself had to learn to take responsibility for a great deal of everyday work. We had timetables for washing up the dishes, we had special areas to clean besides our own rooms and we also did some washing ourselves. I've learnt from that, that everyday work at home is something every family member ought to share equally and one should not regard unpaid work at home as just women's work. My experiences of work at home probably helped me in my first employment, as a deputy male nurse at a mental hospital. I was expected to clean as part of my duties. Many of my female co-workers also, of course, influenced me, especially concerning gender equity. Views on gender equity were stressed even more by my female classmates during my teacher education. My wife is also very conscious concerning these questions. All this contributed to my standpoint as pro gender equity, and I try to integrate it in my teaching. In my opinion, democracy is about anti-hierarchal and anti-authoritarian relations, which clearly include equality and gender equity. I was trained to become an inter-mediate-level teacher between 1974 and 1976 and since then I've worked as an intermediate-level teacher in different classes. Half of my time has been taken up by teaching music. My big interest is music and for many years I have been playing in an amateur band during my leisure time.

(teachers' report: 81)

This is how Lina describes her class in the teachers' report:

My new first grade pupils knew each other well, since most of them had spent the year in pre-school together. One of the pre-school teachers, also the mother of one of the girls, told me that the children got on well together . . . When they started school, I found that this was indeed the case and that the children did get on very well together. There were fourteen girls and nine boys. Seven of the girls were highly visible and independent. The others were more shy, cautious, and more anxious. I had a feeling that they were afraid of doing things wrong. To my know-ledge, none of the girls were leaders of the girls' group. Two of the girls seemed to be unpopular, and interestingly these two girls had not come from the same pre-school group as the other girls. The boys' group was overall easy to handle. They were kind to each other. Two of the boys were particularly visible . . . Compared with the two parallel groups, this group seemed the most harmonious. At the beginning of the school year they were already able to listen to each other without interrupting. A majority had really wanted to come to school and to become edu-cated. But some of the boys were 'too young'. These boys considered other things to be more important than schoolwork . . .

(teachers' report: 26)

Viktor did not explicitly describe Lina's class, but the following are his reflections about individuals and groups:

When working with pupils in music education, my choirs and rock bands, I have asked myself how much a group influences individuals as well as other groups. Through my work I have been in contact with many different kinds of groups . . . My experience is that many indi-viduals' behaviour can be explained by individuals' positions in differ-ent groups. This is why, for example, some girls in some groups don't do themselves justice . . . In order to understand girls' and boys' behav-iour in classrooms, individually and in groups, and to be able to under-stand the matter of creativity, visibility and go-ahead spirit, as well as matters of opposition and conflict in and between these groups, each group has to be treated separately . . . In this school girls seem to be more integrated into a group than boys . . . They want to create a feel-ing of 'we'. 'We' means so much to the girls that they sometimes seem to oppress their 'me' . . . However, in this lie true democratic values, which the girls' group can later develop into competence for gender equity . . . The boys, on the other hand, seem to be more oriented towards individuals . . . I want to stress that this discussion is about two common strains, two ideal type models of girls' groups and boys' groups. In reality there are of course examples of flat structured boys' groups as well as hierarchical girls' groups, and one group can also change depending on activities . . . Cultural patterns and conditions under which these pupils live have resulted in one model being more frequently used than the other by the groups.

(teachers' report: 82ff)

Lina

When Lina selected a sample lesson for observation she chose a mixed-sex technology lesson. The pupils had previously been taught technology in single-sex groups but now Lina wanted the pupils to realize that girls can be as good as boys in the subject. She aimed to:

Use a system of five different laboratory stations, with pupils working in small single-sex groups in the same classroom. I can't say there is a red thread [a Swedish metaphor for a clear aim] concerning the content. It's about making things from drawings and instructions. Gender equity is important in technology. The aim is that the girls will gain self-confidence in technology and the boys will become aware of and respect girls' abilities in the subject. The exercises also include more 'girl-centred' tasks, such as working with dolls' houses.[2]

Like Helena and Lars (see Chapter 5), Lina did not wish to make explicit her message about power relations and gender equity. This lesson accorded with these principles. She hoped that the pupils would implicitly become aware of gender issues. This was her main strategy from the beginning of the project. Below is an extract from her first project paper:

The content includes easy tasks with air, water, heat, electricity and three-dimensional constructions. I have chosen the content with reference to what I think children meet in everyday life. I especially want the girls to open and investigate different electrical apparatus, so that they can investigate what they look like inside and in extension also understand how they work. Girls possess abilities if they just have opportunities to try. I want to encourage a break in the gender patterns, so that girls understand that technology is something also for them.[3]

How did Lina position herself with regard to the pupils in the classroom? Towards the end of the first year the children were asked to describe to a fictitious new classmate the most common features in the classroom – by means of choosing between nine statements. The boys expressed great satisfaction and had no complaints at all. The girls also expressed their satisfaction with their female school-friends, their teacher Lina and schoolwork. However, almost every girl also complained about the boys and their behaviour.[4] Lina responded as follows:

> I don't make explicit who the bad boys are. I want to built on every child's constructive and sympathetic attitudes. Therefore it is important for me to really try to understand and to adjust myself to those pupils who have problems. I work extremely hard with those pupils at the beginning of junior level. It's especially boys I have had to work with. That's also why I want them [the boys] to implicitly become aware of girls' abilities in technology and my position as a female role-model in a masculine subject.[5]

She described how she has attempted to deal with the problems highlighted by the girls:

> We have talked about good and bad leaders. One of the boys . . . has as usual a little 'court' of docile sympathizers in his wake. Since he is a leading figure, and since this is not the first time things have happened, I decided to talk to him in private. This boy is very verbal and he tried in different ways to put the blame on his sympathizers . . . I had the feeling that he did not answer my questions seriously and I had difficulties in getting to grips with him. But when I asked him if he knew someone he admires very much and wanted to be like . . . It was as if I touched a critical point – he suddenly had tears in his eyes . . . 'She [the one he admired and wanted to be like] always listens to me and always takes me seriously', he said. 'Could you imagine yourself as such a leader?', I asked him. 'Yes', he said. Our discussion came to an end and I have never, since then, had any reason to talk to him in private because of bad manners.
>
> (teachers' report: 29)

At the beginning of the project Lina's rationale for selection of content in technology is a common topic of discussion. If she wanted to choose content from children's everyday life, which children was she thinking of? She was encouraged, by the project participants, to think of content more appropriate to girls' everyday life. Lina was also influenced by bad experiences on an in-service course in technology, which encouraged her to rethink the content of technology. For example she criticized 'courses in technology for having too much of a technological bent and not taking into consideration girls' everyday experiences'.[6]

In the lesson selected for observation, Lina included what she considered girl-centred tasks, such as making their own doll's house, making tapestry hangings, laying down lino and lighting lamps. She did not explicitly stress gender issues. However, over the years Lina held to her standpoint, which was to educate girls to become prepared to prosper under 'men's conditions' and in 'masculine' territories.

Lina and Viktor

According to Lina, seven of the girls in her class were independent and prominent, while the rest were much more shy and cautious. Lina believed that all girls need to express their feelings and opinions and therefore she tried different exercises in how to argue and how not to give in simply because someone seems angry. One of the best exercises, according to Lina, was when single-sex small-group discussions were organized with another teacher as a group leader and the form teacher as an ordinary group member, but where the girls chose the topic of discussion themselves.

As mentioned above, Viktor was also involved with the shy and more inhibited girls. Viktor began to work with Sara in Lina's class in a music therapy session with drums. He described how he aimed to contact what he called the girls' 'spontaneous strings inside them' and how he could help them to express themselves by using the drums. He believed he could contribute to making the shy and quiet girls more spontaneous and confident by taking part in such an activity. The following is an example from work with Sara in Lina's class:

> The girls had one thing in common, they played very quietly and cautiously on the drums and deadened the cymbals as soon as there were sounds from them . . . Sara now and then jerked, as if she was frightened. At first I couldn't find a reason for that. Later I discovered that she jerked when she thought she was playing wrongly. I started to wait for such moments, and when she played unintentional double-taps on the cymbal . . . I asked her to play just those double-taps, as if they were practical achievements. This is an important phase in my method. As early as possible I try to transform 'faults' into developments of the music and by hooking into the girl's way of playing I proceed together with her through improvisation. After a while Sara became more relaxed.
>
> (teachers' report: 109)

According to Lina, Sara's behaviour in the classroom changed during this process: 'She is more confident and risks expressing her own opinions. She seems to have gained a higher status in the class and the most visible proof is that she has more friends . . . Now she even questions some of the boys' rules, much to their annoyance' (teachers' report: 112).

Towards the end of the project Lina claimed that both she and the pupils now felt that the girls were more favoured in the classroom. According to

Lina the pupils asked questions like: 'Why do we continue with this gender equity project, when the girls in this class grab the space more compared with the boys? And I answer: Even if it is like that in our classroom, we have to learn that it is not so everywhere.'[7]

Summary

Lina claims that she was not at first interested in the project, since she regarded herself as a teacher who always takes into consideration individual children's needs. When joining the project Lina developed a gender equity strategy, mainly in relation to the subject technology. During the first years Lina stressed the importance of girls' gaining familiarity with and confidence in what is considered to be a male area and under men's conditions. She regarded herself as a positive female role model in technology. During the process she changed lesson content to include girl-friendly exercises connected to girls' everyday lives. However, she tried not to make gender issues explicit and aimed to use gender-neutral words in her teaching.

Lina argued that moments of equity occur when girls gain self-confidence in men's territory and under men's conditions – as in technology – and when boys recognize girls' ability. She used single-sex groups to increase girls' self-confidence in technology. To make the boys aware of the girls' progress and abilities, however, she used mixed-sex groups in the last year. She cooperated with Viktor, who used music therapy to encourage the shy and quiet girls to express their feelings. In order to deal with girls' feelings of discomfort with the boys, Lina talked to the boys in groups as well as individually. Her strategy was not to blame but to develop boys' soft and constructive qualities.

Lina's girls

When interviewed after the technology lesson the girls echoed Lina's message. For instance, they said:

Girls are not just able to take care of children.

Girls are also able to do joinery and to repair cars.

When we are grown-ups we'll be able to do these things.

When asked about gender, they presented a long list of responses which showed awareness of boys' dominance. The girls are very talkative. They express the same complaints as they did one year earlier.[8]

Lads are troublemakers. They fight and such things. They try to be tough guys.

And they scuffle a lot with the girls and the girls surrender but the boys don't surrender.

And they [the boys] always take decisions.

How did they deal with the troublemakers? The girls said they dealt with the boys in two ways. Some acted autonomously:

Girls must also decide for themselves.

Girls must also try to be tough girls.

Others walked away:

I just walk away.

'When the lads decide to put an end to trouble they have caused the girls': here is one example of the girls seeing moments of equity in the classroom. In other examples they echoed Lina:

Everyone should have to put their hand up if they want something.

And not just sit there and babble at the same time all at once.

When interviewed, the girls indicated knowledge of men's power in working life:

Women usually have lower salaries compared with men.

Men decide how much pay you will get.

Men think girls are foolish, therefore they [girls] are not given high salaries.

They suggested two distinct ways of reaching moments of equity at home. For example, some of the girls suggested turn-taking and sharing chores:

Take turns with everything.

Work with the same tasks.

You should do the cooking and cleaning together.

Others argued that certain jobs should be done by boys:

Lads have to repair the car. Girls don't want to do that.

If you are single you either don't have a car or you go to the garage.[9]

At the end of the last semester at junior level they were asked to describe in short written essays what they had learnt about gender equity. The majority of the girls (and the boys) indicated that men and women should collaborate at home and that both boys and girls should do care work. They also knew that they are capable and therefore should not be afraid of doing things they have not done before or of telling other people what they are able to do. Additionally, technology was ranked by the girls as a very important subject. They learned from Lina that:

Boys and girls know an equal amount of technology.

Technology isn't just something for boys.

Girls are also able to do technology, if we want to do it.[10]

Lina's boys

When interviewed after the lesson in technology, the boys described the different exercises they had been working with. When asked if the lesson has anything to do with gender equity, they seemed confused. However, finally, the boy who was considered the brightest boy in the class said: 'This has to do with equity, because girls are learning technology. Usually only boys know about it.' When asked further, the boys said that moments of equity occur when people 'are kind to each other'. For example: 'When one remembers not to shout out' or 'When we are not talking at the same time all at once'.[11] When discussing their relationships with the girls in the class, the boys argued that the girls had learnt how to exert power in the classroom, and they gave over twenty examples of such behaviour (see also Chapter 4). Contrast this with what they had said one and a half years before:

This project is only for the girls.

Boys mess about with the girls when we are together.

This project is for the girls, because they don't dare to challenge us.[12]

What were these boys' interpretations of gender equity in adult life? After the lesson in technology they answered: 'Everyone should do everything.' They gave examples from their own families:

My daddy does the cleaning and cooking more often than my mother does.

It's the same with my father!

But the rule of everyone doing everything clearly cannot always be followed, according to the boys. Gender equity can therefore also mean doing what is most suitable in a situation:

Concerning who is going to take care of the baby, it depends on who has the best job. The person who has the highest salary must go to work.

And it is impossible for us to breast-feed.[13]

When they described what they had learnt about gender equity, they mainly gave the same answers: that men and women should collaborate at home and that boys should do care work.

I made a doll and learnt how to sew. I enjoyed myself and I now like sewing. Boys should know how to sew.

We did a role play about a family. We were supposed to learn that there should be a fair division of labour at home. But I already know that, because that's the way it is in my family.

In their stories about a weekday in the future, they noted that men will take on more housework and leave less for their wives to do. While they said they appreciated Lisbeth's care work lessons, the boys chose Eva's lessons in creative activities as the most important part of the project.

I have learnt that everyone is capable of doing things, if you just decide what you want to become good at.

I have learnt how to dance with girls and I have learnt to dare to do things I haven't done before.[14]

Summary

Lina's technology lessons were ranked by the girls as the most important for gender equity at school. They learned that technology is not just for boys and they knew that girls are able to do joinery and repair cars, for example. There were no explicit statements from boys regarding girls' competence in technology. However, implicit in the statements from boys who argued for sharing work equally in the household is girls having some knowledge of technology too. The girls were aware that boys often dominate situations at school, but they tried to handle the situation with various strategies. Some of them argued with the boys, while others just turned their backs on them. The boys said they had noticed a change in their position in the classroom, since the girls had learnt to challenge them. Moments of equity occurred, according to both girls and boys, when individuals behaved thoughtfully towards each other. When the girls gave examples of what they meant, they all referred to obedience to Lina's rules. While Eva's creative activities had most importance for the boys, the girls also appreciated these lessons. The main message was that Eva stressed the fact that everyone is capable of doing anything.

Both girls and boys discussed moments of equity for adults, primarily in relation to division of labour at home. They stressed the importance of a fair division of labour, and both boys and girls expressed two ways of relating to that statement. One way was to share equally; another was to share work in relation to what is most suitable and what one really needs to do in the situation. The boys did not discuss paid work in relation to gender; however, the girls were aware of the unequal hierarchy and the norm of male superiority.

Siv's classroom (10–13 year age group)

Classroom context

Siv: I am 42 years old, married and mother of a son of 12 and a daughter of 10. I've been working as an intermediate-level teacher since 1975, with breaks for special education and parental leave. I've worked at this school since 1986 and I also live in this little sawmill and archipelago society. My biggest interest since I was a child has been badminton. I started to play actively when I was 13 years old and when I grew older I worked as a coach and a manager at local level as well as at district level. In my sport activities I came across questions concerning gender equity, in particular when we tried to find ways to keep the girls involved in sport when their involvement in athletic contests was finished. The boys stayed as exercise-players and they trained themselves to become coaches. The girls seldom wanted to train themselves, not even to a basic coach level. Even if we, at the time, tried hard to find a solution to that problem, we never did so. When I think of this now, I understand that people working in the sport movement have boys' demands and needs as their norm for work. They don't listen enough to girls and therefore they don't take into consideration girls' demands and special needs. My father was a 'house-husband' for about ten years, because of protracted asthma, and since I was a lonely child and in addition a 'father's girl' we spent a lot of time together. He often stressed the importance of education for women, as one way for us to become independent and stand on our own feet.

(teachers' report: 64)

Valdemar takes woodwork and metalwork in all classes at intermediate level:

I was born in 1942. With the exception of some years during the 1960s, I have grown up and lived in this neighbourhood. At the time of writing this I am 53 years old. I started as a craft teacher in woodwork and metalwork in 1966 and I've been working in this school since 1970. Three crises in my life could have encouraged me to work in this gender equity project. The first occurred when my father became disabled after a bad accident, and I was given a great responsibility for practical work, since I was the big brother with three younger sisters. The second occurred when I got custody of my two young daughters after a separation. I didn't want them to be 'disabled' by having only a man as a model. Cooking, darning stockings and machine sewing therefore became everyday work for me in our home. The third occurred when my youngest daughter died, after being ill with cancer for three years.

Since my oldest daughter was an adolescent at the time, life confronted me with difficult choices . . .

I never had the feeling of a revolution when craft became involved in the gender equity pedagogy project. That could be explained by the fact that I have been through a couple of educational changes in relation to the subject craft. Some of our earlier thoughts about single-sex groups in craft were similar to our discussions in the project group. Therefore, a short retrospective. The 1960s: during my first years as a craft teacher boys primarily had woodwork and metalwork and girls had textile craft. However, there were opportunities to try the other sex's subject for twenty lessons . . . The 1970s and 1980s: at the beginning of the 1970s, there were sympathetic attitudes towards coeducation in craft and it was compulsory for boys and girls to take an equal amount of woodwork and metalwork, as well as textile craft . . . Both sexes got an insight and necessary knowledge in a subject which had previously been a traditional male or female craft. One step towards equality was taken . . . In coeducated groups there are always tensions between the sexes . . . Just the opposite of what is usually expected, sex-segregated boys' groups are much more moderate and calm than coed groups. A boy does not have to make himself important in front of the girl he likes . . . The work in the room becomes more effective . . . In coed groups you always run a risk that boys take over and help girls with, for example, drills and other tools, and the girls never learn to handle them . . . The opposite situation prevails for boys in textile craft.

(teachers' report: 77ff)

This is how Siv describes her class in the teacher's report:

In my class there were thirteen girls and ten boys. Most of them had known each other since early childhood, because their parents simultaneously built and moved into houses in the same area at the same time. The parents were of similar ages and many of them were friends. The boys had sport as an interest in common. Almost everyone played football and during grade 4 basketball became of great interest. The girls' group had also been relatively intact through the years, but, contrary to the boys, they didn't have any prominent common interest. They had different leisure activities such as football, dance, riding, gymnastics. The girls were often together in larger groups and not in friendship relationships. Often, groups with relations like that have a more considerate climate. People don't have to run down others in order to keep their best friend. The girls looked after each other. They were seldom on bad terms and they raised the alarm if someone was hurt or badly treated by the boys. None of the boys in my class had a friend to whom he could talk about emotional matters. A teacher creates keen ears and group solidarity if she builds her pedagogy on showing consideration and respect for others. However, you always take a risk with such a pedagogy. Group solidarity makes the groups very strong. I think group solidarity can be difficult for a teacher, especially during the pupils' adolescence, if difference of opinions occur between a teacher and the pupils.

(teachers' report: 65)

When describing her class, Siv stressed group solidarity. Viktor agreed:

In Siv's class everything goes quickly and easily, but it's not because the pupils are bound by authority. The boys' group and the girls' group are equally strong. They are very interested in music. They tolerate and respect each other and therefore get on well with one another. I think there is a tremendous atmosphere among the pupils, because they like each other. There is a lot of incipient love going on between boys and girls.[15]

Valdemar concurs: 'The group is extremely nice.'[16] Lars also gets on well with the pupils: 'They are sweet and nice. One is happy to be with them. They give you feedback, you get inspired by them and you can be yourself.'[17]

Siv, Viktor and Valdemar

Siv was the form teacher in Lina's former class. Lina and the way she dealt with her pupils at the junior level set a good example according to the inter-mediate-level teachers. Lars noted that Lina was one of his favourite role models.[18] Siv stressed the fact that she and Lina had similar opinions about pedagogy.[19] When asked to select a lesson for observation, both Valdemar and Viktor chose a lesson with Siv's girls. All of them chose to work in single-sex groups. According to Siv, Viktor and Valdemar, gender equity pre-vailed when gender boundaries were crossed, when girls and boys trained and developed competences usually associated with the opposite sex. Let us listen to their arguments.

Siv discussed two lessons in Swedish that took place in single-sex groups:

The girls need to practise oral argumentation techniques, because I real-ize that these girls have difficulties in expressing themselves orally, especially if they have to do it alone, and especially if they have to stand up for an opinion in confrontation with other persons' opinions. The boys need to be able to put words to different expressions of feelings, both orally and written. They do not have as wide a range of words as the girls have.[20]

Viktor discussed a lesson with the girls' rock band:

I want them to cross the 'normal' female boundaries. I'm teaching them to play on instruments that 'normally' count as male; for ex-ample, electric bass guitar, electric guitar, drums. If they learn to cross these boundaries, then hopefully they will not be afraid of crossing other boundaries. I think playing in girls' rock bands is one way of strengthening girls' self-confidence in 'male' areas.[21]

Valdemar discussed a lesson with the girls in woodwork and metalwork:

This is about equity, because . . . my experiences are that in mixed-sex groups only boys take responsibility for the machines . . . the drill, for example. The girls are a bit frightened of these things, while the boys tackle the machines without any self-doubt whatsoever. Boys consider themselves to be more skilled and the girls give up and let them take over. You remove these tendencies in single-sex groups when the girls have to take matters into their own hands.[22]

Lars had similar arguments in relation to boys' education in home economics.

None of the intermediate level teachers in the project explicitly focused on gender power relations in the classroom. In an early interview, Siv explained:

The truth is filtered into them without them recognizing it. An example of success using this method is that only girls expressed their interest in becoming representatives on the school council. Even if the tradition is to select one boy and one girl, the boys trusted two girls to be their representatives.[23]

Viktor preferred referring to gender equity as 'justice':

If we define communication between boys and girls in terms of justice, I believe we will get much better results in practice. This is a better way than trying to make them conscious about gender. My experience is that the boys give space to the girls, when I argue in terms of justice. Boys become convinced that it is fair to let girls get a chance too . . . This is my experience in all three project classes at intermediate level. If a boy discovers he is about to interrupt a girl, or if another boy discovers what he is doing, the first boy usually says something like: 'OK then. Oh, yes.' And the girl will gain the right to proceed. The boys remind each other and I feel that this emerges from our discussions about justice.[24]

Neither Siv nor Valdemar and Viktor explicitly highlighted gender equity and gender relations during the observed lessons. They dealt with gender equity in their actions (see also Chapter 5). Viktor said: 'It will take some time before the girls can start to play. I want them to get the electric instruments in good working order by themselves.'[25] In Valdemar's workshop the girls appear busy doing different things. The following is a quote from the observers' notes:

Valdemar is busy discussing their different work, but he never takes over their work. All the girls seem to be familiar with the different machines and other tools. One is working with the larger drill, another with the grinding-machine, a third is using the small electric fretsaw, a fourth is tidying up the dust from the grinding work with help of suction apparatus, while the rest are busy working with other tools, as Valdemar advises a girl to countersink a little bit more. The girl countersinks as a matter of course.[26]

Neither Valdemar nor Viktor drew attention during lessons to the fact that these groups were girls' groups. Siv agreed with this strategy:

Pupils should be treated not as boys and girls but as whatever group with their special demands and needs. I mean, if you highlight and stress differences between the sexes you conjure up conflicts and the boys need to show their dominance. You should not expose pupils' signs of weakness. It's better to encourage the competences without them noticing what you are dealing with.[27]

During Siv's two observed lessons, the girls practised argumentation techniques by arguing for or against owning a dog, and the boys discussed feelings like joy, anger, sadness, fear and anxiety. Siv began the girls' lesson by repeating the concept of power and Berit Ås's five ways of exercising power (see Chapter 2). She asked the girls to give concrete examples of how these can appear. Siv also asked what feelings those techniques created for the victims. During these discussions the girls themselves raised gender issues. Siv wanted them to be aware of these means of exercising power, but she stressed that they should not be used against others in discussions:

One should not ride roughshod over others by using the techniques of exercising power. These are dirty tricks. It is better to argue in favour of something, to express better counter-arguments to convince others . . . I have to give reasons for why I think it is good to have a dog. I must develop my arguments.[28]

Siv

We have presented some common strains in the three teachers' implicit ways of trying to cross gender boundaries. In the following we describe how Siv tried to derive advantage from any incipient goodwill in the classroom. Siv tried by her own actions to encourage the more sensitive boys during single-sex lessons. The following description from the observation notes provides an example:

The boys are coming into the classroom. Siv: 'How is it Daniel? Have you cut your hair?' She passes her hand over his hair. Daniel: 'Yes' . . . Siv passes her hand over a boy's head while he passes her. He looks contented . . . Siv: 'It's difficult to describe, why one becomes moved and affected. By the way, what in fact is a feeling? Give an example!' No answer. Siv: 'Patrik, you have just mentioned one.' Patrik: 'When one is dying.' Siv: 'How do you mean? In what way?' Patrik: 'When it is tragic or deadly funny . . . Peter: 'Or it could be funny comments. As in *Terminator* . . . Siv: 'These are experiences. For example when you are feeling happy. Those of you who have been happy because of a film, change places!' Everyone change places . . . Siv: 'Those of you who have cried because of happiness, change places!' Daniel: 'On Christmas Eve, when we were to cut a Christmas tree and there were squirrels in the fir. Then I was happy and cried.' Siv: 'Mmm. I bet you entered into the squirrels' feelings, into the world of squirrels.' Jonas: 'In a film about a dog. Then the dog died, but left twenty small puppies. I cried but was still happy that some of them survived.' Patrik: 'On Christmas Eve . . . Siv: 'If you get really frightened; How do you feel?' The boys give suggestions: 'Shaky, like tears, sweaty, shaking tooth, shaking knees. I have to do a poo-poo.' 'Me too.' Siv: 'There is a name for that feeling: a nervous stomach. What is the difference between fear and agony?'[29]

Siv held on to her strategies throughout the project. The first interview focused on some steps in her pedagogy: for example, her way of placing the pupils in pairs, with a girl sitting next to a boy. This could be construed as disadvantageous to the girls if they were used to help teachers and to silence boys. Nevertheless, Siv continued to seat the pupils that way, because she believed that the advantages compensated for the disadvantages:

The pupils have been seated with the same sex before and they have become tired of that. I have also become aware that some of the girls have been left out of the girls' group. The key to belonging in the group seems to be the degree of popularity with the boys. To give the girls with lower status a certain cachet I place every girl next to a boy. Then every girl will become recognized by every boy, since we change places every week according to a system. That gives all pupils the opportunity to come close to their favourites of the other sex. During single-sex lessons we talk about how to behave towards one another. The boys will learn the importance to a girl of being taken seriously and the importance of not patronizing her. In my experience girls with low status have blossomed.[80]

Siv continued with this way of seating her pupils because:

Relationship exercises are keys in my pedagogy and I want to use the 'incipient love' in the classroom to create a cosy atmosphere during mixed-sex lessons. If someone is badly treated I immediately take charge of the situation and talk to those involved in private. I ask each of them: How did you feel when . . . ? The other must listen, explain himself or herself and apologize. I call this an empathy exercise and this is also central to my pedagogy.[31]

Siv's strategy of using 'incipient love' was discussed in the project group. Eva argued against this strategy and Viktor also highlighted the danger of using the power of attraction without being conscious of one's own weakness for the other sex:

> I don't think female teachers are aware of how they fall for the boys. Male teachers are not such easy victims of boys' charm. The boys cannot take advantage of male teachers in the same way. It's the same with me in relation to the girls. I have to really be careful not to fall for their charm, especially when I am with the girls in the rock groups.[32]

Summary

Lina and her way of relating to the pupils at school set a good example, according to the teachers at intermediate level. When Siv takes over Lina's pupils there is a mutual understanding between the two of them. In discussions about gender and gender equity in the project group Siv and Lina most often agreed with each other and disagreed with Eva (see also Chapter 4). According to Siv, Viktor and Valdemar, moments of equity occurred when contextual gender boundaries were crossed. They wanted to cross gender boundaries without the pupils noticing what they were dealing with. Siv often used single-sex groups for different gender-sensitive exercises. Viktor and Valdemar arranged single-sex lessons in order to enable the girls to become familiar with tools and instruments usually connected with males. Viktor consciously used the more gender neutral word 'justice' instead of 'gender equity', because he believed that the pupils have more positive associations to the word justice. To limit conflicts between the sexes in the classroom during mixed-sex lessons Siv tried to create a cosy, even heterosexual, atmosphere by taking advantage of the 'incipient love' between girls and boys. However, Viktor sounded a warning, arguing that adults need to be aware of their own feelings and weaknesses for some pupils, and he was supported by Eva.

Siv's girls

In the interviews directly after the observed lessons with Siv, Viktor and Valdemar, the girls identified connections between content and equity when Siv was teaching:

> This is about equity [no hesitation, all agree].
>
> We will learn how to argue . . .
>
> Yes, we'll learn how to talk and to answer for ourselves.
>
> So that we don't just put up with all that rubbish.

But the girls were disappointed with the content.

It should have been something other than owning or not owning a dog!

I hope during the next lesson we will be able to discuss: why is it good to be a girl? [agreement].

The connection to equity was not as obvious in Valdemar's and Viktor's teaching. The girls made tentative suggestions: 'There is equity in the single-sex groups because perhaps girls are encouraged to develop in woodwork and metalwork.' They discussed whether biological sex differences have anything to do with girls' capability in woodwork and metalwork or in textile craft:

I don't understand why it should be that girls are good at sewing and needlework and boys at woodwork and metalwork. I mean it could be quite the reverse. I prefer to work with wood.

Yes, I am really bad at needlework.

No, I prefer to do needlework.

Some of the boys are really good at textile craft.

Yes, I like the gloves they made.

Regarding the girls' rock group run by Viktor, they observed:

This can be regarded as equity because we ourselves have decided to create this rock group.

It's not Viktor who wants us to play. It's us who have demanded these lessons, because we want to learn how to play rock together.

Now we are doing it the way *we* like. I mean, girls can show that they are skilled in music.

Yes, it's not just boys who are clever.

During the interviews the girls revealed that they were aware of boys' ways of trying to dominate in the classroom, but they also gave examples of how they had changed the situation for the better. Some of them declared that they had put an end to the boys' oral harassment.

Earlier the boys used to call us whores and such things.

They really did it . . . spoke it out.

And if I say, 'Why don't the girls have the same opportunities as boys do?', then they [the boys] call me: 'Bloody feminist!'

Yes, and they say they are anti-feminists without even knowing what that means. If they really knew, they would mean that girls must take on the whole burden of unpaid work and they can't really mean that. I don't think they do.

But this was earlier . . . They are not like that any longer.

I think the girls in our class are good at putting their foot down now.

Others told us that they had put an end to the boys' ways of claiming space.

For example if they are sitting on your desk, slapping and scuffling about . . . earlier we just were quiet or in a squeaky voice said stop it. Now you really shout at them.

If you put your foot down seriously, they become quiet.

And now there actually are more boys that sit quietly compared with girls.

They also realized that they were of great value and much coveted.

I think our boys really got the message . . .

. . . that girls are not worthless.

It's up to the boys now. It depends on them now.

They have to realize that if they want to keep us as friends and girl-friends, they must . . .

. . . They must learn that they can't keep us if they behave boorishly.

They stressed the value of single-sex education.

I think the single-sex groups have really been a help for our progress.

Equity in the classroom was prevalent, according to the girls, when:

Boys take girls seriously. All that we say. It's not just that we should have equal opportunities to speak up. The boys must also take what we say seriously – this really is a serious matter.

But it's not just the boys. The teachers should also act in a more equitable way.

Equity is when boys and girls are told off by a teacher for the same reasons.

These girls argued for greater equity in the classroom. In fact, they didn't regard Siv as sufficiently feminist:

She is nice, but she is so strange. The boundary of what is acceptable in the classroom is much more extended for boys.

Yes, if a girl opens her mouth, she gets told off immediately, while the boys can chat for a long time [nods of agreement].

As when Peter did a handstand . . .

. . . Yes, he did a handstand and she didn't say anything . . .

. . . And he was standing up against her desk!

They suggested that closer monitoring of classroom activities was needed:

You should put a camera in the classroom without anyone knowing it. Then you would see what is really happening.

Some of these girls expressed disappointment because they didn't feel they could talk to the female teachers about their experiences:

The female teachers. I think they have some difficulties in . . .

. . . Some of them, not all of them, don't understand that girls should have the same possibilities and rights . . . as the boys get.

We have tried to take these things up with Siv, but she doesn't listen to us.

These girls said they got more support from their male teachers: that is, from Lars, who supports them, and from Viktor, whom they respect.

I actually think Viktor is the teacher who takes the most active part in this equity project.

No, that must be Eva.

They ended up agreeing that all the teachers had some commitment to gender equity, but Viktor and Eva took it most seriously.

When asked to describe the classroom climate, the girls commented: 'We keep together. Nobody is left outside the group.' Thus, although they recognized that some positive changes had occurred, they wanted things to go further. For example, there were still things to do in the girls' group:

Some of us who were very quiet at the junior level, we have started talking much more in grades 4 and 5.

Yes, you express what you want to do more now, but still I think girls are rather uncomfortable about claiming more space for themselves.

The girls also argued for changes in leisure activities: 'In sport there are also glaring injustices. There is a lot of money invested in ice hockey, while almost nothing is invested in horse riding.'[33]

Again, as with the other groups, they saw equity in adult life as concerning sharing domestic tasks and equal access to paid work.

Equity is when you do an equal amount of cleaning, washing up the dishes, cooking and everything like that.

Not only men should chop wood.

Not only mothers should wash up the dishes.

Equity at home is when male and female do an equal amount of work and when both consider it to be fair.

> I consider the best for males is to learn how to cook, for example. It's good that we are in single-sex groups in home economics, so both boys and girls can . . .

> . . . Yes, you have to know how to do it.

Some of them were aware of the unfairness of who did what in their own families, and they wanted to change that pattern in their future families.

> But it's not like this in my family at home. My elder brother doesn't do a damn thing at home, but I have to lay the table and to clear away and I'm the babysitter.

> It's unfair, but from the very start girls are brought up to be sweet and nice and boys to be rowdy.

> I will not treat my own kids like that, because now that I have come this far I realize that I don't have to bring them up in my parent's way.

In terms of paid work outside the home:

> Equity is sharing equally.

> To have equal rights.

> Everyone should have equal salaries.

> If we in this rock band get paid, we should have the same salary.

> When they were asked what they wanted to do as a career the most popular job was 'police'. Some also mentioned being therapists, two of them 'therapist for sexual abused children' and 'therapist for anorectic children.' Other suggestions included:

> Work in a zoo or something like that, an actress or at a daycare centre, something with theatre or art school, painting or dancing, veterinary, to work in a shop or something with art.

> I'm in fact rather interested in technology.

> Perhaps something in a laboratory.

> I would like to be active in building something up.

Clearly these young people were considering careers which cross the gender divide.

These girls seem unusually confident and proud of themselves: 'I don't think girls, when fighting for equity, should become like boys, because girls have certain good qualities like being good listeners and we can talk about sensitive things and such like and that is something boys have to learn from us.'[34]

When we look back across the data, we can see few changes in the girls' expressed views about equity. However, their last essays about an ordinary day in a future life can be interpreted as protests against the conventional nuclear patriarchal family and as expressions of creative and challenging alternatives. Nearly half the girls did not portray themselves as living in a nuclear family. Described ways of living include: being single as a rich and famous musician, having a lesbian relationship, being a widow or a single mother with children, having a family with children and a home-husband and living with a man but having no children.

The essays suggest that these girls had insights into the strength of patriarchal society and the patriarchal family, and the risks which may exist when challenging this way of living. The stories have dark sides too, containing descriptions of suicidal thoughts, alcoholism and being cast out of society. They tell stories about wives in ordinary families having headaches as a result of overwork, both inside and outside the home.[35]

Siv's boys

Siv selected as the lesson for observation with the boys a single-sex Swedish lesson with group discussions, which was similar to many others conducted during the project. It was clear that most of the boys found such lessons enormously valuable. The following are examples from written essays at an early stage of the project:

> It's wonderful to be together with just boys. You can talk about everything.

> To talk with boys is rewarding. You are able to tell if you have been teased or bullied and there are no girls laughing behind your back.

> It's easier to have things out if there are just boys.

> You get peace and you dare to do more things.

> I want more discussions about relationships and more lessons in Swedish.[36]

Some of the boys mentioned home economics and care work as among the most rewarding lessons offered to single-sex groups:

> You make food you are proud of and no girl is there to criticize you.

> I want more home economics. I want it once a week.

> I like home economics, because we learn how to cook and to bake bread and much more.

> I especially liked when we learnt to sew our own dolls at the junior level. It was good to learn how to sew.[37]

However, in spite of the fact that the boys had stressed the importance of single-sex discussions in their early essays and had given both the teachers and researchers the impression that they appreciated these discussions during the process, they seemed embarrassed and hesitant when asked to discuss the observed lesson with the researcher. There was a long silence after the first questions, concerning the aims of the observed lesson, before they hesitantly replied:

Perhaps she [Siv] just wanted to ask for our opinions.

We don't know.

It was about feelings [giggling].

I don't know.

There was another long silence while the boys looked at each other. Then:

I don't know. I don't think she has any aims at all. She never has [hesitant laughs; the boys are looking at each other].

I never know if this is about school knowledge . . . She has done this a lot of times.

Yes.

And I don't care.

This is at least more fun than sitting and working with maths or something or English [nod of agreement].

After some discussion of gender equity in the classroom, one of them exclaimed: 'This is even more difficult!' But one of them answered: 'Gender equity is when all of them are coming to you' (nods of agreement). This statement refers to Siv's rotating system of placing the pupils in the classroom in different boy/girl pairs. When asked to describe situations in which a good atmosphere prevails, they returned to the single-sex boys' groups:

That's when it's just boys in the classroom.

Then it's a good climate, because all of us are discussing what has been going on.

These boys had different opinions on Siv's aspirations concerning gender: 'She doesn't like any rubbish.' Some of them thought the boys were treated unfairly: 'When we are in single-sex groups everything is OK, but as soon as we are together with the girls and we start to babble, she at once just goes "shush, shush!"' Others thought themselves to be favourites: 'But still, if she is sitting at her desk reading, I can do a handstand, without her really bothering. If this had been Lars, he would have said, "Sit down immediately!"'

They agreed that the person who had most power in the classroom was Siv herself. Siv inevitably got things her way:

Yes, our teacher must have been educated specially in how to talk people down.

She always talks us down.

She finds loopholes to do what she wants.

Equity between adults was again seen as existing when domestic tasks are equally shared:

Both are working in paid work.

Yes, no housewife.

Well, it should actually be like this, that both are doing an equal amount of unpaid work.

You always want to do as little as possible of that work, don't you? It's not especially fun to clean the floor, vacuum, scrub the toilet and so on.[38]

Four months after this, just before they were leaving the intermediate level, the boys were asked to write about a school day and what they might have learnt about gender equity. Some of their comments indicated both criticism of the teachers' strategy on gender equity and a wish to learn more about gender equity. Of the thirty lessons described, just over half said little about gender equity.

Criticisms include a lack of clarity on what equity means. 'Single-sex groups in sport have something to do with the gender equity project, but I don't understand what exactly.'

The boys' selections of lessons were interesting, because male teachers were overrepresented. Twenty of the thirty lessons contained a male teacher. Most popular were home economics with Lars, sport with a male teacher (not participating actively in the project), the single-sex choir with Viktor, Lars's lessons in English and Swedish, Viktor's activities connected to music, the single-sex camp with Viktor and Lars, and Valdemar's lessons in craft. However, computer work taught by a female teacher (not participating actively in the project) on an hourly basis was also mentioned as one of the most popular lessons. Comments included the following:

We have home economics and we learn how to wash up the dishes and things like that which a lot of people think only girls can do.

Today is the last performance of our musical 'Boys and Girls in Our District Today and Yesterday'. We have done some research and we have interviewed people of different ages to learn more about women's and men's lives in our district.

In a single-sex group we act out girls' roles in a serious way. We are supposed to enter into and learn how it is to live a life as a girl.

In some lessons we learn to give girls space and not always claim space for ourselves.

We are on a camp where we learn about sexual matters and living together – about girls' thoughts and their lives.

We have single-sex groups in craft in order that nobody laughs when a boy is sewing the wrong way or a girl cuts her finger when doing woodwork.

Lessons in computers are probably divided into single-sex groups so that we don't get upset when we find out that the girls are more clever.

When the boys described an ordinary day in the future the majority expected their lives to be different to their own parents'. Only four boys imagined living in a nuclear family. Six boys imagined living alone but one expected to share his life with a dog and a woman he loves who doesn't live with him. These boys anticipated that they would be involved in cleaning up, doing the dishes, shopping and cutting the grass. Only one boy described himself as taking part in activities with his children. Three other boys imagined having children, but the children were at school during the day.

Thus the main ideas expanded in these essays could be interpreted as a protest against a patriarchal nuclear family, with the suggestion that one way of achieving gender equity is to live alone and to avoid having children. Half of the group indicated that paid work was not a matter of course in the future. They described how they tried to get casual jobs to get enough money to enjoy the good life, which includes sport and leisure activities. One of them mentioned that he would need a gun. However, the jobs they suggested for themselves were rather stereotypically masculine, such as sport star, coach, electrician, motor vehicle inspector, odd job man. More gender-neutral jobs include zookeeper and comic strip artist. Most boys emphasized fun and adventure.[39]

Summary
In accordance with the teachers' aims, both boys and girls, but especially the girls, expressed wishes to cross gender boundaries. Siv's girls were critical of gender boundaries connected to biological sex, since some of them were interested and more skilled in 'male' subjects. The boys also expressed the wish to cross gender boundaries, but in more implicit ways: for example, by stressing their appreciation of single-sex lessons. Even if the situation had been changed for the better, the girls wanted greater gender equity in the classroom. Restricting equity issues to 'equal opportunities' was not enough

for them. What they wanted was for their demands to be taken much more seriously and for the boys to realize that they had things to learn from girls. The girls felt proud in being female and aimed to keep together and support each other in the classroom. Their main obstacle, they argued, was not the boys or the male teachers but certain female teachers, especially Siv. The girls were critical of Siv, because they did not find her explicit enough concerning gender relations. To reach moments of equity in the classroom, they claimed, Siv had to change and take girls' claims really seriously. The girls were particularly satisfied with the support they gained from the male teachers, especially from Lars and Viktor, and they also highlighted Eva's clear and strong commitment at junior level.

The boys, on the other hand, had difficulties in explaining what gender equity in school is all about. Segregation seemed to be the most obvious solution to them. They also approved of Siv's way of placing girls next to boys in the classroom according to a set rotating system. However, the boys seemed to have mixed feelings about Siv's way of relating to them in single-sex groups. They valued her way of supporting them but they, like the girls, were critical of the fact that her lessons lacked explicit gender-sensitive content.

For both girls and boys moments of equity in the society outside school meant sharing equality and having equal rights. The girls also had insight into inequalities in society in general, highlighting, for example, gender inequality in leisure activities. Indeed, there were times when both girls and boys seemed to reject the concept of the nuclear patriarchal family. The majority of the boys and about half the girls expected their lives to be different from their own parents'. Some girls stressed that they had learnt things from the gender equity project that were different from their parents' ways of acting. When talking about the future, most of the boys and some of the girls appeared to seek to solve gender matters by aiming to live on their own or by preferring to stick with their own sex.

Reflections

There was considerable agreement about what constituted a gender equity pedagogy among the teachers in the two classrooms. The most positive outcomes of the teachers' strategies were that both girls and boys were perceived as being kinder to each other, and that the girls were not afraid to claim their own space. Both boys and girls greatly valued the contribution of the single-sex lessons.

However, the paradox is that, despite the considerable agreement on pedagogy among the teachers, data from these two classrooms have been ambiguous and difficult to interpret. The teachers' claims that the children get on well together in the classroom and that the girls' and the boys' groups are both strong were confirmed by our observation notes. However, these claims were not entirely sustainable in the light of the younger girls' complaints about the boys, and the older girls' complaints that female teachers were too lenient to boys. Female teachers' leniency to boys was confirmed by our diary, interviews and some observation notes. However, the female teachers' adaption to the boys' needs was often aimed at increasing equality between the sexes, since the teachers simultaneously tried to develop the boys' sensitive and collaborative qualities. They tried to influence the boys to become more understanding of females' needs and female values.

Siv's and Lina's (and Lisbeth's) reactions to the girls' complaints were to reject them. The women teachers argued that the girls, especially Siv's older girls, merely wanted to be at the centre of every situation. From the research data it is clear that Siv's girls were active and sought attention, but this occurred only when they attempted to put gender on the agenda. They seemed to have to struggle to be at the centre of attention, in order to counteract the male norm culture in the classroom. On the one hand, the male teachers supported the girls' viewpoint; on the other, Siv and Lina (and Lisbeth) resisted the girls' interpretation. The pupils' essays in these two classrooms also provided contradictory messages. We do not really know whether all that is written should be taken seriously, or should be interpreted as indications of protests or as jokes. We, as researchers, found support in our data for all these apparently contradictory claims. Nevertheless, we suggest that both descriptions are 'real' in these classrooms. Siv's girls, for example, may be correct in accusing female teachers of being opposed to them. At the same time, they may be seeking attention, as the female teachers note.

It might be argued that the female teachers took too cautious an approach to the girls and their wishes to challenge male norms in the classroom. It might also be argued that this caution enabled male norms to regain a foothold in the classroom. The male teachers seemed more able to devote their attention to the girls, perhaps because the boys appeared to have greater confidence in their male teachers. It seemed that male teachers were more readily taken seriously on gender issues by the pupils. One reason for this might be the higher status of males and masculinity generally, but another might be the local culture of celebrating male football. Paradoxically, this indicates how vitally important the support of male teachers is for schools working for greater gender equity generally, and especially in sporty cultures.

Notes

1 This short-term temporary replacement post is similar to the position of supply teacher in the UK.

2 Interview with Lina, January 1995.

3 Lina's document, September 1993.

4 Pupils' individual documents, spring 1994.

5 Interview with Lina, September 1994.

6 Researcher's diary, August 1994.

7 Group discussion with the junior level teachers, April 1995.

8 Written documents, spring 1994.

9 Interview with Lina's girls, February 1995.

10 Written essays by Lina's girls, May 1995.

11 Interview with Lina's boys, February 1995.

12 Interview with Lina's boys, October 1993.

13 Interview with Lina's boys, February 1995.

14 Written essays by Lina's boys, May 1995.

15 Interview with Viktor, October 1994.

16 Interview with Valdemar, December 1994.

17 Interview with Lars, November 1994.

18 Interview with Lars, November 1994.

19 Interview with Siv, June 1994.

20 Interview with Siv, January 1995.

21 Interview with Viktor, January 1995.

22 Interview with Valdemar, December 1994.

23 Interview with Siv, September 1994.

24 Group discussion with the intermediate teachers, March 1995.

25 Observation of Viktor and some of Siv's girls in the music room, January 1995.

26 Observation of Viktor and Siv's girls in the woodwork and metal room, December 1994.

27 Interview with Siv, September 1994.

28 Observation of Siv and her girls, January 1995.

29 Observation of Siv and her boys, January 1995.

30 Interview with Siv, June 1994.

31 Interview with Siv, September 1994.

32 Researcher's diary, February 1995.

33 Written essays by Siv's girls, spring 1994.

34 Interviews with Siv's girls, December 1994, January 1995, February 1995.

35 Written essays, May 1995.

36 Written essays, autumn 1993.

37 Written essays, autumn 1993.

38 Interview with Siv's boys, January 1995.

39 Written essays, May 1995.

7 In Lisbeth's and Anders's classrooms: moments of equity

In this chapter we first enter Lisbeth's junior-level classroom and then move on to Anders's intermediate-level classroom. Anders's pupils were previously in Lisbeth's class. When Anders's selected lesson was due to be observed, he was away with a broken arm, so Lars had to take over his teaching. Lars's and Anders's views on how to teach the pupils for gender equity in Anders's classroom are therefore presented together in this chapter.

Lisbeth's classroom (7–10 year age group)

Classroom context

Lisbeth: I've been working as a junior-level teacher since 1962 and in this school since 1974. I'm married and have four grown-up children, two boys and two girls. As the oldest sister of four children I had to take responsibility at home from an early age. It was important in my family to make myself useful. As a teenager I started to work with different children's groups in the Pentecostal Movement's church, something I have continued to do. As an adult I have met boys and girls in different situations on a daily basis: as a mother, teacher, youth worker and in recent years as a grandmother. Every role has difficulties but also pleasures. When we decided to accept the gender equity project which our colleague Eva challenged us with, I felt that the most important task for me was to take responsibility for care work with all the juniors . . . The aim with the education in care work is that both boys and girls should, through practical work, gather knowledge about caring and housework in practice. The main aim is to strengthen the boys' self-reliance in a traditional female area . . . When I was young I thought, if one just educated boys and girls in the same way, there would be equal results. Now I have realized that they have different needs. In education I think the most successful method is to start from every child's individual needs.

This is how she presented her class:

In the group of 7-year-old children, who became my pupils, twelve were girls and ten were boys. About half of the group consisted of a divided pre-school group and the other half came from different full-time pre-school centres. They lived in different housing areas and many of the children didn't know each other. The boys were different from each other in personality as well as in maturity. We therefore worked hard with different contact exercises and discussion exercises. Even though we worked with such tasks, it took a long time for them to settle down. The girls were divided into two groups, one with strong visible girls and the other with silent (but not timid) girls. More recently the boys and girls have got on better together, but the boys still demand too much of my time.

(teachers' report: 31ff)

Lisbeth

Lisbeth selected two single-sex lessons in care work to be observed. As mentioned above, Lisbeth regarded care work as her special contribution to the project.

The theme for this lesson is 'the home'. I want to make visible all tasks that have to be done in a home. The pupils have previously written down what kind of housework each member of the family usually does. They have also been asked to describe which tasks they can do by themselves and which tasks they need someone else's help with. We will start this lesson by discussing these notes. We will highlight what kind of work has to be done every day and every week. I will ask them: What do we do at home? What could gender equity mean during an ordinary day? Are there differences between grown-ups and children in relation to these tasks? A lot of unpaid housework goes on every day in a home. Many people are not aware of those facts. This lesson is a continuation of the more practical education in housework we did last semester. In earlier lessons the pupils have practised washing, cooking and cleaning. Now we are going to talk about these issues. This is about equity, because all of us have to learn how to do our share of housework, so that everyone in a family gets the chance to study and to take part in politics.[1]

The first observed session involved a lesson in the girls' group. Lisbeth started the lesson by telling them about her night duties when her four children were babies. She went on: 'Today you are going to talk about the jobs that you've been able to do yourself and what you have needed help with. For example, when you wake up, do you wake up by yourselves or is mummy the one who wakes you up?' Lisbeth started a discussion about what one could do for other people: 'Some domestic tasks you can do for other people. For example, even if it is me that does the cooking it is for everyone in the family. The jobs you have been able to do on your own, have you done them for other people or just for yourself?' The girls told their stories one by one. Most of the care work the girls had done was for them-selves, while caring for others' needs was primarily done by their mothers, and sometimes by their fathers.

Lisbeth posed new questions arising from the girls' stories: 'If someone has to do all the work at home, do they get any time off? Or does mummy really enjoy washing up the dishes, doing the cleaning, and washing all the time?' The discussion turned towards examples when the girls believed that their mothers really enjoyed housework. According to Lisbeth, housework is important as well as enjoyable, but in her view a mother cannot do all the important housework without assistance.[2]

In the second session with the boys' group, Lisbeth also told them about the nights when her four children were babies. Lisbeth: 'When you become daddies . . . Are you going to get up in the middle of the night to feed the baby with baby food and to change the nappy?' The boys: 'No.' Lisbeth: 'No?' Lisbeth left the subject and turned to another issue.

However, she tried other ways to raise the importance of housework. When one boy said, 'But Mum does the cooking,' Lisbeth commented: 'Yes, you have seen what really happens, that it is usually mothers who do the cooking. Even if you are not a baby any longer and can eat by yourself, someone has to do the cooking for you and the rest of the family every day.' She prompted the discussion about helping others around the home: 'Is it good that children should help', she asked, stressing the importance of chil-dren making themselves useful.[3]

During these two single-sex sessions on housework, Lisbeth most often focused on differences between adults, especially mothers, and children. In other sessions, Lisbeth focused on the father's role. In commenting on some of her pupils' pieces of writing and on classroom observations, Lisbeth said:

> The boys have to be trained to take on more responsibility. I sometimes say, 'This is not mummy's homework.' If someone has left his home-work at home, he has to go home and bring it back to school. One mis-take tends to be enough; next time he will remember it. The problem is, though, that there is no one at home . . . I have suggested education for parents.

Lisbeth's view, reiterated many times, was that parents should do what she called 'more caring work in the home and less work and leisure time outside home'. When attention was drawn to the fact that Lisbeth's reference to a parent tended to be the mothers, Lisbeth corrected herself: 'Well, I mean both mothers and fathers.' Her main method of solving problems at school was to involve the parents. She often talked about a special education for parents. Her problem was that the parents did not come when she asked them. She believed that they did not come because 'the vast majority of the parents are completely absorbed in their work and their own hobbies'.[4]

Thinking of her present class and recalling her former pupils, her impression was that the girls at the start of the intermediate level were brighter and more successful and independent, while the boys were more excitable, vivid and childish.[5] During the project, Lisbeth has been keen to encourage the boys to take on more responsibility for themselves and for others and, in order to encourage caring feelings, she let them sew their own mascots. This was an idea borrowed from a Norwegian project, where early efforts to teach boys to care for dolls did not work at all, since the boys handled the dolls roughly. However, when the boys handmade their own mascots, they showed more caring attitudes towards them (Ve 1992). Lisbeth and her colleagues used these handmade mascots in different role plays and, according to the teachers, the boys took care of them in lesson time and break time. Inspired by the Norwegian teachers, Lisbeth also invited parents with babies into the school, so that boys had the opportunity to hold and care for babies. During these sessions the parents discussed maternity and paternity leave and rights with the children.

Lisbeth commented on how she dealt with the division of labour at home: 'We talked about equity and how we all have to be capable of dealing with the full range of work that has to be done at home.' When asked to be more specific about what she meant by the division of labour between mothers and fathers, she answered: 'I don't think we have to be good at everything, females and males can complement each other.' She had, it seems, two contradictory viewpoints on what the division of labour means: (a) that men and women should be capable of doing similar tasks; (b) that women and men should complement each other. Her response was: 'Well, I am in fact more in sympathy with the view that we should complement each other. I haven't stressed the fact that we need to share the work on a 50–50 basis, because I don't think we should do that.'[6]

Lisbeth's main message during her years of work with the children was to stress the importance of a female caring culture, focusing on the mother and her duties. Another key message has been the importance of supporting people who need help in Sweden, as well as people in other countries. 'We are in the decade of the individualists. I would like to see more discussions in the classrooms and among us participants in the project group about consideration, caring and esteem'.[7] According to Lisbeth, this was something she stressed in her teaching at school, as well as in the Pentecostal Movement.[8] Lisbeth also initiated the work on the United Nations' Children Convention in the school (see Chapters 2 and 5).

Lisbeth very seldom took an active part in discussions about the relations between gender differences in paid work, politics and leisure activities. She left this to the other teachers. Her activities were instead related to caring for other people's needs, family questions and unpaid work. She was also practically oriented at project meetings, where she always made coffee, despite the fact that there was a rota for coffee making. She never, as the other female teachers did, commented if she helped a male teacher with coffee making. Her behaviour indicated pride in being a woman and suggestes that she saw it as a superior 'calling'.

Summary
Consideration, caring and esteem were keywords when Lisbeth discussed gender equity and educational issues. Lisbeth initiated work with the United Nations' Children's Convention by stressing the importance of global caring. Her view was that the way to reach equity in society is to spend more time caring for each other in the family, and she believed that, in order to increase equity at a global level, Swedish people needed to become less individualistic and more caring about the fate of children in other countries. She decided to take the main responsibility for teaching care work to all the juniors, with the aim of educating the pupils, especially the boys, to adopt the norm of consideration, caring and esteem. She offered the mother as a role model to show the children how to make themselves useful in relation to each other in the classroom and at home. Since she believed that girls and boys have different needs, Lisbeth organized her teaching in single-sex sessions for this topic. She also wanted to include parents more and to cooperate with them more. However, she was disappointed in their response, since the parents did not seem to want to cooperate with her. She was not sympathetic to the individualistic life of many parents, who appeared to spend a lot of time in paid work or occupied in leisure activities. Instead, Lisbeth preferred a complementary way of life, with housewives at home doing the necessary care work for the whole family and men being the breadwinners.

Lisbeth's girls

After the observed lesson the girls discussed Lisbeth's message with the interviewer:

We should learn how to make ourselves useful.

And what has to be done at home.

Yes, so that mummy and daddy don't have to do everything.

When asked about their understanding of what gender equity is in practice, they all talked about collaboration in different ways:

That is collaboration.

When one lends a hand and makes oneself useful.

When not only one person has to do everything.

One should collaborate at home.

They discussed relationships between children and adults, especially mothers, but some of them were hesitant about them sharing work equally with their mother: 'I think that the mothers should do more than the children, because when children become grown-up they will also have to do more than their children. But of course, in spite of that, one should learn to do these tasks.' The discussion turned to the importance of them learning housework for a future: 'If children don't do any work at home, then they will not learn how to do housework, and then they cannot live on their own when they are adults.'

The girls appeared very occupied by mother–children relations. Consequently, it was difficult to make them focus on gender relations between women and men. They had to be asked directly. The first to answer the question suggested that equitable collaboration is 'If a father mends the car, because the mother cannot do that, and instead the mother does the ironing and washing.' Immediately, others objected to this interpretation: 'There will be less work for men then, because cars don't have to be mended that often.' The discussion continued over the apparent implication that this necessarily implied less work for men. Some argued that many girls are also good at and like mending cars and therefore that could be seen as part of housework. These girls did not like the complementary perspective in gender equity at all:

Equity, that is that everyone does an equal amount of everything.

For example to take in turns doing all tasks every two days.

The discussion ended with a suggestion that parents should decide for themselves what interpretation of equity to use.

If the girls had different opinions of what equity means for adults, what about equity between boys and girls in the classroom?

That is when we are kind.

Yes, and when we consider others' needs and aren't so selfish.

And it is important that the teacher treats boys and girls equally.

When asked whether there were equal relationships in the classroom, they give different answers:

No, the boys talk too much.

When the boys are there you are afraid of expressing yourself in the classroom.

They laugh and make fun of us . . .

. . . And roll up their eyes to heaven like this.

However, some girls disagreed and stressed that gender equity was a feature of the classroom:

But I think we have equal space to talk.

Our teacher says, that the boys work as well as we do when they are in single-sex groups.

We chat as much as the boys do when we are together.

Yes and they [the boys] talk so loud and disturb Lisbeth, so that we can talk a lot without the teacher recognizing us doing it, because the boys speak so loudly.[9]

From the project data, it is clear that the girls knew that single-sex groups were being used to eliminate the disturbance of dominating boys. 'It's quiet and calm when the boys are away and we work better without the boys.' The girls were also aware that they were supposed to cross gender boundaries.

Boys are supposed to learn girls' things and girls to learn boys' things.

Boys are supposed to learn how to take good care of babies.

In the course of the project the girls learned that they need to cooperate in different ways and to make themselves more useful. They also ranked care work and knowledge about housework as the most important issues raised by the project. They all described themselves in the future as combining housework with paid work.[10]

Lisbeth's boys

The first things that crossed the boys' minds when they were asked what they were supposed to learn from the care work lesson were:

To learn how to help oneself in life.

We are supposed to learn to do housework and not just lie down and have a lazy time.

When asked if this knowledge had anything to do with equity, many of the boys thought so:

You learn that you are able to make yourself useful at home.

This is about how we will be able to help ourselves as grown-ups.

I like equity. Do you know what we did during the craft lesson? We embroidered.

When the questioning was turned towards views on equity between boys and girls in classroom practice, the boys immediately replied: 'Kind.' And then, more specifically:

I know what it is to be kind. If someone is sad one should comfort that person.

Yes, one should be friends and not quarrel.

If one is nasty to another the other should stay kind, because the first then will stop being nasty . . . after some years or so.

One should not tease the girls.

And the girls should not tease the boys.

Yes, the girls shouldn't kiss the boys [laughing].

The boys had more to say about Lisbeth's opinions on boys and girls:

She wants us to be kind and decent.

And not fool about and chat all the time.

When asked if there were equity relations in school, the majority answered: 'Yes.' But some boys said: 'But sometimes the girls tell us off too much.' Others said: 'Both boys and girls tell each other off at times.'

As to equity in adulthood, the boys' views differed here too. The majority thought it meant sharing paid work and housework equally:

Both of them should be in paid work.

And both should take care of the baby.

Otherwise they will start quarrelling and get angry with each other.

If only one of them does everything, they will probably get divorced.

Yet others considered equity to be prevalent when a woman and a man complement each other:

The mother could do the washing while the father mends the car. There are not many girls who train to become car mechanics.[11]

At the beginning of the project, the boys considered it to be aimed at making both boys and girls more sympathetic to each other, and felt that both boys and girls misbehaved, but there was less of a problem in single-sex groups.[12] One boy, John, supported by some others, even asked Lisbeth to help them to act more equally:

After a very noisy lesson . . . the boys were the main culprits . . . Lisbeth breaks off the lesson, even though it is not yet time for the ordinary break. She asks the pupils if they have any ideas why she has stopped the lesson. A discussion between Lisbeth and the boys starts. John suggests what should have been done: 'You shouldn't wait for us to stop by ourselves. You should immediately have a go at us when we behave badly.'[13]

(This example could of course also be regarded as a moment of normalization, if John was trying to blame the female teacher for his and the other boys' domination in the classroom by demanding that she take responsibility for it.)

Like the girls, the boys thought that equity pedagogy was aimed at 'Teaching boys "girls' things" and girls "boy's things".' They also acknowledge the importance of care work: 'It's important to be capable, when you are an adult and have your own kids.'[14]

At the end of the project the boys continued to consider care work to be the most important element in equity, believing that they had now learnt how to make more of an effort at housework.[15]

Summary

The pupils in Lisbeth's classroom agreed with Lisbeth that gender equity involves both school and home. Both girls and boys stated that they had learnt that they should not be selfish but instead make themselves more useful at home, be sympathetic and caring at school and consider other children's needs. However, there were also clear differences. The boys more often than the girls used the expression 'to help ourselves', indicating that they were not to be so demanding of help from others. In contrast, the girls more often than the boys used the expression 'collaboration', indicating their focus on cooperating on different tasks in different situations. Both girls and boys regarded care work as the most important subject related to gender equity, and both stressed the fact that they needed to learn about housework in order to be able to live as equal adults. Echoing Lisbeth, they provided two suggestions of how equitable relationships at home could be realized. One is the complementary way, where women and men do different tasks. The other is to share tasks, by, for example, taking turns. In both the girls' group and the boys' group different opinions emerged on how they were affected by the other sex in the classroom. Some girls felt ridiculed or restricted in space by the boys, while others argued that they had an advantage and more space to do what they liked, since Lisbeth was occupied with keeping her eyes on the boys. The majority of the boys claimed that the class was equitable because the pupils had developed caring attitudes to each other. However, others suggested that the girls told the boys off too much.

Anders's classroom (10–13 year age group)

Classroom context

Anders: I'm 46 years old. I'm married and have two children, a girl aged 21 and a boy aged 18. I have worked as an intermediate-level teacher since 1972. In 1976 I started to work in this school and I have been a member of this working team since 1983. I'm interested in questions connected with unions. I am a representative of the Swedish Union of Teachers at this school and the head negotiator in this school management area. Sport has been and still is my main leisure pursuit. I have been an active sportsman in football and bandy. My own active sport career ended when I was 30 years old. I carried on as a football coach in both boys' and senior teams. For the last ten years I have been coaching a boys' team and I have had the opportunity to follow their development from the age of 8 years old until they became seniors. It has been a pleasant, interesting and exciting period of my life. The reason why I started to train a boys' team was because my son was that age. At the same time my daughter was training and playing basketball in a girls' team. A reflection from that time is: when coaching a boys' team I felt a lot of support and interest coming from the other parents. They watched the matches and it was easy to persuade them to give the boys a lift to the matches in other places and relatively easy to get financial support to purchase equipment etc. At the same time I realized how very few parents there were who took part in and supported the girls in the basketball team. I asked myself: could it be that boys and girls experience sport under different conditions, not just according to public contributions and support but also according to their parents' support?

Gender equity became a way of life for me after 1971, when I started living with my wife, probably because of the experiences we have both had through growing together. Moreover, my wife's parents had a very equal relationship. In 1974, when my daughter was born, I was on paternity leave for three months. At that time I was one of the pioneers who utilized the right to shared parental leave at child birth.

This is how Anders described Lisbeth's former pupils:

When I took over from Lisbeth there were nine girls and twelve boys. Four of the boys were newcomers. During the three years at intermediate level there were additional newcomers but also some children left. In grade 6 there were twelve girls and nine boys in the class.

In grade 6 four boys practised football, two of whom were also playing ice hockey. One of the girls practised swimming several days a week and a group of six girls played badminton once a week. Three of them joined the sea scouts. Besides, many pupils were interested in animals and many also had their own pets.

The characteristic of this group was that the girls set the tone. The girls were more go-ahead and visible, they were more obviously knowledgeable and dexterous. The differences in maturity between boys and girls that usually occur at intermediate level were clearly visible in this group already in grade 4 and were even more obvious in grade 6. When the number of girls exceeded the number of boys, the girls' position as the stronger group was consolidated.

There were also visible differences compared to the usual pattern in boys' groups. There was no apparent leader in this group. The most mature boys in the group were simultaneously quiet and a little shy. They kept a low profile as a whole, particularly in relation to the girls. The boys who were more go-ahead were at the same time the most childish ones, who took their own personal needs as their starting-point instead of the needs of the whole group. Often the boys' actions were silly: for example, in attempting to become the class clown. From an early point, the girls showed tolerance of the boys and the girls always showed enthusiasm during common activities with the boys, such as parties, disco and dancing exercise during music lessons.

One specific feature of this class was a girl with impaired hearing in both ears, who wore hearing aids. We naturally made special arrangements for her. The classroom was adjusted, with hearing loops put around the walls and acoustic boards in the ceiling. All teachers wore special microphones . . . In grade six the boys realized that they were in the minority and the question is whether that had a negative influence on them during decision-making. A united girls' group was always impossible to vote against.

(teachers' report: 60ff)

Lisbeth described her former class thus: 'These girls were already very strong at the junior level. It was therefore important for me to support the boys. They almost disappeared in the classroom.'[16] Anders in general agreed that the girls were more advanced. So did the other teachers at intermediate level. This was, for example, Viktor's view: 'It's easy to work in Anders's class. The girls rule the classroom. They like dancing and the boys get inspired by the girls' initiatives and therefore I let them practise dancing every third lesson. Our system is that girls and boys take turns in asking a partner to dance.'[17] As was the case with the other teachers at intermediate level, Anders delegated some of his lessons to Lars, who taught Swedish, English, natural science and home economics. Lars also confirmed the girls' relative strength: 'At the intermediate level girls are, from a general point of view, better in oral English compared with boys. These differences are most marked in Anders's class.'[18]

Anders

As already mentioned, Anders was away with a broken arm when our observation of one of his lessons was scheduled. Lars took over and in the next section we present his plans for the observed lesson. Anders's views on equity are also presented, taken from previous interviews, discussions and observations. Since Anders had the main responsibility for the class, his views are presented first.

As already stated, Anders was very engaged in the Swedish Union of Teachers and saw one of his main tasks in the project as developing a gender-sensitive educational method that would help to develop skills in dealing with practical political work. He called his method 'negotiating play'.

> The aims of negotiating play are to make the pupils conscious about gender questions of current interest and to teach the pupils how to take sides and how to argue in favour of their opinions, to listen to other people's opinions and perhaps to revalue their own opinions. I got the idea after having participated in a course for union representatives. We learnt what a readjustment negotiation is and how to negotiate in small groups. Back at school I realized that this could be something useful in the gender equity project, since the question of gender equity in policy means that females and males should have equal opportunities to participate in political and union matters on equal terms.
>
> (teachers' report: 62)

The principles of negotiation play are, briefly:

1 Negotiate in small single-sex groups on the issues that you later want to get accepted in a mixed-gender negotiation.
2 When agreement has been reached, find suitable arguments to support this position.
3 Select the persons who are to represent the whole group in the final mixed-gender negotiation.
4 Carry the final negotiation through.

Anders introduced into schoolwork negotiations about the legal aspects of gender equity, job evaluations etc. Basic data for these activities include statistics on women and men in Sweden, which are regularly updated and published by the Swedish government (Swedish Statistics). (See also the example presented at the beginning of Chapter 5.) Anders noted that the boys and girls in his class used different means to accomplish their aims in the negotiation plays.

> The girls do not choose the most verbal and confident girls as representatives for the final negotiation. They always draw lots. Consequently, they all have interest in backing and encouraging each other. And all of them feel fit for the challenge. This is not the case in the boys' group, where a lot of them lack confidence in the challenge. There are usually just one or two who volunteer to be representatives.

Anders considered the girls' way of working as the best way: 'From now on I will try to encourage the boys to use the girls' way of drawing lots to avoid the hierarchy system among the boys.'[19]

Another example of how Anders adopted girls' way of working can be seen in a Swedish lesson. It started with a discussion on what the pupils had been doing during the lunch break. As mentioned in Chapter 4, football is a major interest in the district and both pupils and teachers often discuss football or other competitive sports, such as basketball or ice hockey. However, Anders's girls were not especially interested in playing competitive games themselves during the breaks. They preferred non-competitive games, such as skipping or hopscotch, problem-solving games or just talking to each other. Anders made a great effort to adjust himself to the girls' interests as observations from the beginning of one such lesson show:

> Anders: 'Now you have had a break for lunch, how was it?' Some voices: 'Good!' Caroline moves to the notice-board and starts to fasten a map with pins. Anders looking at the girls: 'Did you skip?' A girl's voice: 'Four of us.' Anders: 'What did the rest of you do?' Caroline answers him from her position by the notice-board: 'We played hopscotch.' There are no objections or additional comments from the boys. [Some of them probably joined the girls' games, as they often do.]

The lesson continued with Anders reading a book about love and relationships (Pohl 1991). As the research note describes:

> Anders starts to read a book about a young, Swedish girl Malin and her boyfriend Gurra. But before he starts, Anders wants them to remember what happened earlier. 'What was the previous chapter about?' Erik puts his hand up and answers: 'She started to cry.' Anders: 'Why did she start crying?' A boy: 'Malin thought Gurra would not care about her any more, after what she had done.' Anders goes on describing, in his own words, Malin's feelings. The girls who are usually most active in commenting and asking questions are sitting at their desks listening to Anders with dreamy [researcher's comment] eyes . . . Anders: 'What does Malin do?' Kent: 'She cuddles Gurra.' Anders: 'And more?' Sven: 'She whispers in Gurra's ear and asks for forgiveness.' Anders: 'Yes, don't you think a person who can ask for forgiveness is a strong person? She is great, isn't she?' Kalle says: 'And Gurra says to Malin, "Damn, how I like your perfume".' They discuss the value of 'damn' in this very situation.

The leading character in this book is Malin, and her feelings and experiences are explored. Anders especially involved the boys in discussions about the content. The lesson continued with oral reading exercises, where Anders divided the class into small mixed-sex oral reading groups. These groups were sent to work all over the school building. As usual, the girls took up leadership roles in the reading groups, while the boys asked them for help, listening to their comments and following their advice.[20]

On the whole Anders was proud of his class and the way they related to each other. He gave the girls credit for that. 'My class don't ever talk badly about other pupils. New pupils and the girl with hearing disabilities are well cared for in my class.' Viktor agreed, saying that he saw many more cliques and 'hidden' status hierarchies in the other classes. Helena also agreed, pointing out that none of Anders's boys had bad manners, like some of hers: for example, in pushing themselves forward all the time. Anders praised his girls again: 'There are no quarrels among the girls.' Lars: 'Yes, in those cases when I decide whom they are going to work with, the girls in the other classes always have some objections. Anders's girls, however, have the opinion that it's beneficial to work with someone you do not know well.'[21]

There were other aspects regarding the boys' way of working which Anders wanted to change. The content of the boys' essays made him quite indignant. For example:

Anders: 'In my class the girls write more modest everyday stories, while the boys pile up a huge number of actions, the more bloody the better. I don't like them' [the boys' stories]. Eva asks how he might break this pattern. Anders: 'Perhaps forbid the boys from writing such stories.' Lars often chooses the exercises himself: 'I have given them the same exercises in single-sex groups, but they usually turn out different, because the girls are more advanced.' Eva asks if the girls should not get more advanced tasks if they are so much more clever. Lars: 'No, because each turns out differently anyway.'[22]

Lars

At the beginning of the project Lars was impressed by the girls and how they related to each other and to the boys in the classroom. However, as time passed he changed his mind and became convinced that a reversed sexism occurred in the classroom. Lars highlighted his and Anders's different interpretations of the relations between girls and boys, as well as their different strategies for reaching gender equity in the classroom:

One of my aims in Anders's class has been to support the boys and encourage them to express their opinions in public. I have to quiet down the girls, because they claim too much space. They just shout out and dominate the situation, like some boys in other classes do. So, my task in his classroom has been to give more space to the boys and to have the boys express at least some opinions about whatever they want to talk about . . . And I probably try to quieten the girls more than you [Anders] do.[23]

Lars chose an oral English single-sex session for his observed lesson. While three months earlier Lars regarded the girls in Anders's class as outstanding in oral English compared to the boys, he now believed there had been a change: 'Now Anders's class is more homogeneous in English and I could, in fact, educate them in mixed-sex groups.' However, he still used single-sex groups. His argument was that he found it difficult to change the organization in the middle of a semester:

> I will use some of the exercises I have collected in a folder. The two groups will work with the same exercises. It's about daring to express yourself orally in English. They are to work in pairs solving crosswords. One of them, who will get to know the words in advance, will describe what the word is about in English, and the other will guess what the English word is. Another task for the pairs is to describe a picture in English so that the other is able to select the right picture from others. The third task is to write a word and put it on the back of a person. That person is to ask questions in English about that word and the other is just allowed to answer yes or no. This goes on until the word is revealed. The reason why I do this is because everyone in Anders's class needs training in oral English.[24]

Lars did not comment further on gender issues. As described in Chapter 5 with regard to Helena's class, Lars wanted to avoid specific pointers and instead demonstrated gender equity through his actions.

Summary

Anders took over a class where the boys had had more help and consideration from Lisbeth than the girls had. She argued that it was the girls who really had the advantage, and therefore needed less help. Anders, and the other teachers at intermediate level, agreed that these girls were more advanced, and that they set a non-hierarchical, collaborative, caring and supportive tone. Anders had always been impressed by Lisbeth's female pupils, whose ways of working, collaborating and solving problems he found more impressive than those of the boys. Therefore, Anders wanted to attain gender equity by supporting the girls and using them as role models in his work to change the boys' behaviour. Since Anders was a teacher union representative his special task in the project was to teach practical political work. Often, when teaching politics, he used examples which highlighted gender power relations between women and men in Swedish society. However, like the majority of the teachers in this project, Anders seldom explicitly stressed gender power relations in the classroom during other lessons.

While Anders maintained support of the girls in his classroom, Lars became more critical and convinced that the girls had too great an advantage. In contrast to Anders, Lars changed his way of relating to the girls in the course of the project. He thought that equity would be better served if girls' domination was reduced and more space was given to the boys. He also suggested that he subdued the girls more than Anders did. The consequence, he said, was that regarding English the boys had now reached almost the same level as the girls.

Anders's girls

In a group discussion after the English lesson with Lars, the girls did not refer to equity. According to the girls, this lesson was about learning English. When asked directly if the lesson had something to do with gender equity, they asked whether this meant single-sex groups. They knew, for example, that single-sex groups were instituted as a strategy when the gender equity project started. They pondered on Lars's strategies as follows:

He probably thinks that the boys should be more alert in answering questions.

Yes, because it is almost always girls that answer questions. If we are in mixed-sex classes only girls dare to answer questions.

When asked what they think of Anders's strategies, they were silent at first. One girl started to talk, but hesitated to go on. However, the other girls encouraged her to continue:

Well, I don't know but . . . Well, sometimes he is nicer to the girls [some noises of agreement].

Sometimes.

Yes, sometimes.

We girls are actually a little . . .

. . . We sometimes talk too much.

We talk more than the boys do [agreement].

They discussed whether Anders stopped the girls more often than the boys or vice versa. They gave examples of both and found it impossible in the end to come to a firm view. They instead described how they thought they differed from other girls: 'We are not like other girls who just sit like this [the girl demonstrates a passive and well mannered girl] and put our hands up, while the boys occupy space and just shout out answers. We often also do that, shout out the answers, I mean. We seldom put our hands up.'

When asked to describe a classroom, with an ethos of gender equity, they offered the following examples:

You know, sometimes we are working in smaller groups. Then there are perhaps two boys and two girls. We work fairly well together.

It is working *really* well, I would say.

The only subject within which the girls felt that they were not superior to boys was woodwork and metalwork:

But we have woodwork and metalwork . . .

. . . When you do such things [woodwork and metalwork] you would not dare to express yourselves if the boys were present.

You would feel stupid.

When asked if there was still something they would like to change, they suggested the following:

Yes, the boys. When they chat, they just scream and haven't really anything to say.

When we chat during schoolwork, our conversations are more like . . . we are really talking with one another like we do now.

And during the breaks, if we stay in the classroom, we sit together discussing like this, while the boys chase each other around in the room. Things like this.

Our boys are a bit odd.

At least some of them are.

What were these girls' opinions of gender equity for adults?

At home. It shouldn't be like this, that just the man is working [in paid work] and the woman is cooking [unpaid work at home] and so on. I want to change that.

I think girls and boys should have equal salaries. It is often the case that men are given more payment.

For example, there are not as many female car mechanics.

And if a girl trains to become a car mechanic she will be laughed at.

Are *you* a car mechanic?

They gave a lot of examples to emphasize that, independent of sex, everyone has abilities and should be allowed to work with whatever they like. However, they had different experiences and opinions in relation to some jobs:

Well, a girl perhaps should not become a furniture remover. It is too heavy for them.

But there are female removers, you know. When we moved a woman did all the packing. She helped us and the boys lifted the heavy things.

There are not so many male air stewards. I don't think they are interested in that work.

You are wrong. I got so surprised. Once, when I went by aeroplane, a male was the steward.

I think boys should of course become air stewards [noises of agreement].

Yes, and the girls should have the right to become pilots [agreement].

Yes, there aren't many of them.

The girls argued that both Anders and Lars shared their opinions that one should have the opportunity to choose a job independent of sex.[25] On the whole, the girls seemed to like it the way it was in the classroom. These girls and boys expressed enormous satisfaction with the school. Few wanted to change anything and few had complaints:

I like everything we have done.

It is exciting and fun.

Because it is interesting.

I think everything is just good.[26]

The girls described the class as 'Nice and kind, supportive but a little bit too noisy.' Seven of eleven girls wrote that they 'cannot think of any girl either in the class or in the neighbourhood that they dislike'.[27] There was nothing like this in the other classes. Anders's girls seemed to be having a great time at school.

When they looked back and reflected on what they had learnt about equity, they said that girls and boys are of equal value and should have equal opportunities to learn what they need in order to become equal adults:

In home economics with Lars, we have learnt that boys can do the same tasks as girls in a home.

When we learnt how to make a fish dish in home economics, the boys did as well as the girls.

When we have had computer classes, we have learnt that girls can learn as much as boys about computer engineering. We have started to write a 'Girls' newspaper' on the computer.

During computer lessons I have learnt that boys and girls have equal rights and are of the same worth.

During craft lessons we have learnt that it is not only girls who can do things and have the responsibility of patching up and mending things.

Writing essays about the future, the girls imagined themselves in traditional families with children and animals. They would have jobs and share the housework with their husbands. Compared with the other classes at intermediate level, these girls anticipated the highest degree of sharing in housework. Their children, they anticipated, would go to school or to day nursery, except in one instance. Their diverse choice of professions included veterinary surgeon, nurse, doctor, researcher, policewoman and jobs with animals. During leisure time, they expected to watch TV and to take the dog out for a walk.[28]

Anders's boys

The boys, in contrast, considered Lars's main aim to be teaching them oral English. There were great difficulties in getting them to talk about their relationships in the classroom.

'Give examples of when gender equity prevails in the classroom!' The answer was silence. 'Do you think equity prevails between boys and girls in your classroom?' 'Yes.' (Silence.) 'What is it like when equity is a classroom feature?' (Silence.) 'If you had to describe your classroom to someone who was not familiar with it, how would you describe it?' (Silence.) Not until they were asked about Anders and gender equity, did they really start talking. They felt that Anders was not impartial:

He behaves differently towards girls and boys [noises of agreement].

He is nicer to the girls [agreement].

The boys considered they were badly treated:

This is bad.

Sexism.

Blackmail.

They felt that Lars was fairer:

He [Lars] is more just to boys and girls.

Yes, very much more [agreement].

They said they would not mind having more lessons in single-sex groups so that they did not need to be with girls.

It was difficult to get them to talk again. However, when asked about what gender equity means, they responded:

Equal salaries for the same job.

Equity at home is being able to do the same tasks.

Yes, everyone should be involved.[29]

Earlier project data did not indicate disappointment with Anders. As mentioned above, both girls and boys expressed satisfaction with the earlier phase of the project. Then, the boys were more appreciative than the girls of their form teacher's sympathetic attitude. Eight of nine boys described

Anders as a 'good', 'competent', 'kind' and 'not harsh' teacher. Anders was a central figure in their descriptions and none of the other teachers was mentioned there.[30]

Later the boys did not explicitly criticize Anders. However, they made him invisible. The boys wrote that they had learnt that boys are just as good as girls, and that home economics, the camp where they discussed sex and coexistence, and craft were most useful for gender equity.

> Now I have learnt from Lars's lessons in home economics that we can cook and do the same things as the girls can.

> I have learnt from Valdemar that girls can work in wood.

> My opinion is also that girls/women are able and should work more with computers.

> During lessons in textile craft we have learnt how to sew, knit and such things. Today we are going to use the sewing machine again. I have learnt that boys can work in textile craft.

> We went camping with Lars and Viktor and I have learnt about boys and girls and this will be good to know in the future.

The boys seemed family-oriented when describing their futures. They expected to live in families with children, sharing equally in the housework and in caring for the children. The boys saw their leisure time as being spent with the family, with cosy evenings at home if they were not at a restaurant with the whole family. Like the girls, the boys' essays contained a spirit of confidence in the future.[31]

Summary

The girls thought they were different from other girls in the school, since they claimed space and raised their voices without waiting to be asked. Moments of equity were seen to occur when the boys were encouraged to become more like girls: for example, by expressing their own opinions in discussions. The girls suggested that the division into single-sex groups during some lessons was geared to helping the boys to become more lively in the classroom. They also suggested that their classroom had good examples of equitable relationships between the sexes. Both girls and boys seemed to be comfortable in this classroom compared with others. However, at about the same time as Lars switched his attitude to the boys, the boys changed their way of expressing themselves by noting how Anders seemed to favour the girls to the extent that the boys had become the oppressed. They emphasized Lars's work and his courage in supporting them. They implicitly agreed with the girls that moments of equity in this classroom occurred when the boys were supported, so that they were able to catch up with the girls. Experiences in Anders's and Lars's lessons did not, however, seem to alter either the boys' or the girls' belief in equal relationships. Compared with the other classes, girls and boys in Anders's class described a future of more equal family life, in harmony with the Swedish aims of gender equity.

Reflections

As we have seen in Chapters 5, 6 and 7, there is a continuum of ways in which the teachers in the project interpret the Swedish aim of gender equality, with Eva representing one pole and Lisbeth the other. As we have seen, Lisbeth seldom supported the individualistic, competitive norms. However, neither did Lisbeth argue against Eva's opinions. Instead, Lisbeth argued for caring, consideration and esteem, and acted as a role model in this as often as possible.

Lisbeth's and Anders's classes were regarded as having the most 'female culture'. As we saw in Chapter 4, there were times when Lisbeth appeared more lenient to boys' than to girls' demands for help. There were also times when she demanded that the girls pay attention to the boys' needs. Anders's strategy in Lisbeth's former class was to support the girls and their way of acting and solving problems, since he believed that their non-hierarchical, collaborative and caring ways are the most useful for achieving gender equity. A strategy used by both Lisbeth and Anders was to take females as role models.

Unlike the other teachers and the majority of Swedes, Lisbeth had a strong religious commitment. For example, she was highly involved in work for the Pentecostal Movement and saw the Christian commandment to love one's neighbour as going in hand with her strategies for gender equity. Through their work in the Pentecostal Movement and the Swedish Union of Teachers respectively, both Lisbeth and Anders, more than the other teachers (except for Eva), had a broader approach, since they both had clear (although different) ideas of what a 'good society' might imply. For Anders such societies are built on grassroots democratic activities, where everyone, of whatever sex and social background, is involved, while for Lisbeth they are caring societies built on Christian values.

It might be questioned whether Lisbeth is a feminist at all, since she showed a preference for men and women having different roles in society. It could also be argued that her views contradict the Swedish concept of equality, which stresses similarities between the sexes. However, using Olive Banks's (1981) broad concept of feminism, Lisbeth's concern with social issues – for example, her concern to stress the importance of global caring and her work with the United Nations' Children's Convention – and her commitment to the Pentecostal Movement accord with the feminist tradition of evangelical Christianity, which, according to Banks, has links to radical feminism. The links, however, are built on emphasizing differences between the sexes, at the same time claiming women's moral superiority. As we have seen, Lisbeth certainly believed that women are morally superior. However, in her teaching she highlighted the importance of boys learning care work. Her aims in teaching about care work lay in a hope that both boys and girls, as adults, would spend more time caring for people, whether at a local or global level.

The middle-class girls and boys reacted different to Lisbeth's and Anders's teaching. According to the teachers involved in the project, the girls became mature, strong and successful, whereas the boys remained noisy, childish and too demanding. It seems that Lisbeth's and Anders's strategies worked well for the girls but less so for the boys. In fact, the boys' situation became more problematic, as they not only failed in their schoolwork, but were excluded and frozen out in their relations with other boys and girls of the same age, because the boys were regarded as too childish and immature. Since this was a common feature of many classes that had Lisbeth as a class teacher, it might be argued that Lisbeth's greater lenience with boys had encourage the girls to develop, but restricted the eventual development of the boys.

Both Anders and Lars found the boys' situation, which became more problematic in grade 6, unsatisfactory. However, they did not agree on how to solve the problem. As we saw in Chapter 4, Anders wanted to involve the other teachers in supporting the boys, while maintaining support for the girls. However, Lars and the other teachers of the class were more conservative and tried to normalize the situation by identifying the root of the problem in the boys themselves, rather than in their own resistance to girls' successful gender crossings. Lars, who decided to interpret the situation as reversed sexism, started to clamp down on the girls, while encouraging the boys to think about their unjust position in the classroom. As a consequence, Lars argued that the boys were able to reach the same level as the girls in the English language, implicitly confirming that the policy of reverse sexism had been successful. However, the same English lessons showed incidences when Lars had to negate girls' wishes to solve exercises in their ways. It is arguable whether Lars's methods of dealing with the girls really caused improvements in the boys' schoolwork.

At the end of the project, it was evident that the girls had retained confidence in their capabilities and their futures, but there was still no solution to the boys' frozen out position among other boys and girls of the same age.

Notes

1 Interview with Lisbeth, December 1994.
2 Observation of Lisbeth's lesson with the girls, January 1995.
3 Observation of Lisbeth's lesson with the boys, January 1995.

4 Interview with Lisbeth, November 1994.
5 Observation notes, April 1994.
6 Interview with Lisbeth, April 1995.
7 Researcher's diary, September 1994.
8 Interview with Lisbeth, November 1994.
9 Interview with the girls, January 1995.
10 Written essays, May 1995.
11 Interview with the boys, January 1995.
12 Interview with the boys, October 1993.
13 Observation in Lisbeth's classroom, October 1993.
14 Interview with the boys, October 1993.
15 Written essays, May 1995.
16 Observation notes, April 1994.
17 Interview with Viktor, October 1994.
18 Interview with Lars, November 1994.
19 Interview with Anders, September 1994.
20 Observation notes, April 1994.
21 Researcher's diary, September 1994.
22 Researcher's diary, September 1994.
23 Group discussion with the teachers at the intermediate level, March 1995.
24 Interview with Lars, February 1995.
25 Interview with Anders's girls, February 1995.
26 Written essays, autumn 1993.
27 Written essays, spring 1994.
28 Written essays, May 1995.
29 Interview with Anders's boys, February 1995.
30 Written essays, May 1994.
31 Written essays, May 1995.

8 In support of action research for gender equity

In this chapter we argue that action research is an appropriate approach for increasing gender equity in school. We discuss what we have learnt from being involved in an action research project and examine what the project has meant for gender change in the Swedish context. We also discuss how our experiences have value for teachers engaged in action research in other contexts and why action research is appropriate in a period between the modern and the postmodern.

Five good reasons for action research

The project group has been innovative in Sweden. During the years of work the participants went through a process which changed both our practices and our consciousness about power and gender. Before analysing the results, we briefly review the context in which the project was carried out.

The project teachers qualified as members of the teaching profession at a time when national curricula were highly regulated. As the project was carried through, a new, more deregulated national curriculum was implemented. As mentioned earlier, a shift of school policy in Sweden devolved responsibility for finance and teaching development to schools. The shift also opened up possibilities for schools to create a distinctive image and ethos. The start of the project was the first time these teachers had been really challenged about their understanding of their teaching, and the first time they had been forced to argue for and to document arguments for their ways of teaching. During this period, not only the action research project, but also the greater autonomy and independence of schools, laid an onus on teachers to document and to evaluate their work. Since these two activities were carried through by different and opposite logics, the teachers were left, as Lars commented in Chapter 5, with an almost unreasonable burden of work.

At the time of writing this chapter, the result of policy reforms had just been evaluated (Nationell kvalitetsgranskning av skolan 1998). The evaluators criticize Swedish schools for doing too little to improve pedagogy in the classroom. It therefore seems that the teaching routines developed during the era of rule-governed national curricula remain a strong influence on schoolwork in Sweden (*ibid.*: 44).

The shifts in school policy occurred during a period of increasing globalization of the economy, a greater emphasis on market forces and a gradual erosion of the national and welfare states. Public sector funding is shrinking, which is also affecting the economy of schools. The few schools that have taken the opportunity to create a distinctive image and ethos have done so according to market demands, with an emphasis on natural sciences and technology most common. When characterizing their profiles, these schools often emphasize gender equity and the need for girls' engagement in schooling. As we have seen from the rhetoric in policy documents of the Swedish welfare state (see Chapter 1), women are encouraged to enter 'masculine' areas, while earlier explicit support for men taking responsibility for unpaid work and care in the home has disappeared. Despite these tendencies, project participants chose to highlight both paid and unpaid work and to challenge both female and male traditional gender patterns. This distinctive image of changing both girls and boys is unique in Swedish schools.

When working with the teachers, we were sometimes impatient and wanted more to happen in the classrooms and in the minds of the teachers and pupils. However, in an analysis of the outcome of such a project, it is important to keep the Swedish school policy context in mind. What we learnt from the process of action research is that the frequency of normalizing moments was greater than we at first expected. We also became aware that normalizing power is stronger than we first expected. Initially, we regarded these moments as failures. However, we later learnt that the only way to be able to counteract and deconstruct unequal power relations is to make gender discourses visible. These normalizing moments thus unmasked discursive gender boundaries and enabled us to cooperate to challenge them. The most important point gained from this was that we became aware of how gender power is embodied. That is, we became aware of how discursive patterns rule our own bodies and minds.

These experiences made us realize that our initial optimistic modern vision of enlightment campaigns was inadequate. Real understanding cannot be attained by someone claiming 'truth'. It comes through bodily experiences of discursive and contextual normalizing processes. This provides us with the first reason why this kind of critical action research is important: action research is about learning from actions. However, this kind of work demands considerable time. If change through action research is to be achieved in schools (or wherever it takes place), teachers need more time for inquiry and reflections.

We have also learnt to challenge the distinction between 'theory' and 'practice'; in this case, between researchers working with theories and teachers working with practice in classrooms. As we have seen, collective experiences through actions are the key to better understanding. This is the second reason for using this form of action research: in action research the participants aim to achieve equality in relationships. However, this kind of work also requires a bridging of the gap between teachers and researchers, and the raising of the status of teachers' work. One way of contributing to such a development is to incorporate action research in the education of prospective teachers and in in-service training for existing teachers.

It is clear to us that there is no single 'right solution' as to how to teach for gender equity in schools. Our research took place in a fairly uniform white middle-class context. Despite that, the six classrooms responded differently because of the ways in which the actors chose to position themselves in relation to each other. Power relations appeared in many forms, which also generated a wide range of possible strategies to counteract gender power relations and to teach for gender equity. This is the third reason for this kind of critical action research: action research works at a local level. However, this kind of work demands engagement with people involved at the local level. This is another reason why teachers' duties need to be changed to include more time for action research.

When we became aware that there is no single correct way to work with action research on gender equity, we also became aware of the different and sometimes competing ways of gaining meaning from the same event. As researchers we tended to overstress female disadvantage and inscribe girls and women as victims. Teachers, on the other hand, tended to overstress their freedom for action and by implication to understress the impact of unequal gender practices.

All those involved in the project learnt that one event could embrace many, perhaps contradictory, but nevertheless reasonably reliable explanations. One event could also embrace many contradictory but nevertheless reasonable values. Thus we learnt to regard the event in terms of 'both and' rather than in terms of 'either or' and 'good or bad'. We learnt to grasp the spaces and also the range of opportunities for individuals to act for change, without underestimating discursive power. In other words, we all became aware of how complex and often contradictory a single situation is, and that an event imbues both spaces for individuals to act and obstacles presented by ourselves, living in embodied power relations. We therefore argue that moments of normalization simultaneously offer moments of equity and that moments of equity simultaneously offer moments of normalization. This is the fourth reason for this kind of critical action research: the only way to be aware of the limits of such contradictory forces is to experience them in action. However, this demands collective working and teacher teams which take into consideration pupils' experiences. Action research is one way of creating teams that can act, experience and change their work.

We also note that all those involved in the inquiry (researchers, as well as teachers and pupils) realized the importance of soul-searching and self-reflection. We all attained a greater understanding of the complexity of gender power relations in school and we are better prepared to make normalizing processes visible and to meet them with different solutions. We could never have attained this without being participants in the action research process, and this is our fifth reason for action research: one important method in action research is self-reflection.

Action research for gender change

To exemplify these understandings, let us reflect on what this project has meant for gender change. As we mentioned above, the outcome has to be understood in relation to the context in which the project was carried out. In this case it has to be related to the shift in Swedish school and economic policy.

However, there are also local circumstances, which are of importance in understanding what happened in the different classrooms regarding gender change. We need to draw the reader's attention to the competitive masculine climate and the impact of football in the area. The project school is located in a small village of only 8500 inhabitants, but with two popular and successful football teams. The impact of football appears in many ways, and we want to remind the reader that one of the female teachers (Lisbeth), who grew up in the district, found it impossible in her youth to have boyfriends who supported the 'wrong' football team. Besides being influenced by masculine and competitive values, the school climate is influenced by middle-class (nuclear) families, which have almost no contact with other forms of family. Finally, we highlight a part of the context which should not be neglected when discussing the outcomes of the action research project. We presented the teachers in pairs, since we wanted to see how the ways of working which developed between junior teachers and the junior pupils later influenced how intermediate teachers were able to position themselves in relation to the pupils.

How did the teachers' different strategies influence the possibility of achieving gender equity in the classrooms?

Eva and Lisbeth were the two teachers who were most explicit in their teaching about what they were aiming for. As we have seen, they chose contradictory ways and imagined contradictory societies. While Eva stressed the value of independence and competition in society, Lisbeth most often stressed the value of care work in the home, solidarity and empathy. Eva expressed neo-liberal values and Lisbeth Christian values. Eva tended to be

critical of mothering nurturance, whereas Lisbeth was critical of individualism and egoism. However, since the abilities to care and to compete are
important and not exchangeable according to gender equality, they were
able to understand each other's standpoints.

When Helena and Lars took over Eva's pupils they sought to challenge
Eva's competitive values, and countered with strategies aiming at solidarity
between the pupils. In contrast, Anders adapted himself to Lisbeth's ways of
teaching the pupils care work, but replaced the Christian rhetoric with a
grassroots democracy rhetoric.

The girls seem to have gained in both contexts. Eva's girls, who had to
compete with a large number of boys, felt encouraged by Eva's open support
and thought that they gained more space to manoeuvre in the classroom.
They expressed the value of having single-sex sessions in this classroom in
which boys were overrepresented. However, the stronger positioning of the
girls was challenged as soon as other teachers came into the classroom. This
also occurred when they moved to intermediate level and to Helena and
Lars. Here the boys tried to recapture power and the polarization and tensions between the sexes appeared to increase.

It might be argued that this would not have happened if Eva not had left
the introduction of care work to another teacher. If she had stressed that part
of the concept of equality herself, the boys perhaps would not have tried so
hard to recapture power. However, the largely middle-class girls did not give
up their hard fought positions easily. They kept on defending themselves. It
did not seem to matter that Lars and Helena chose different, less explicit,
strategies for gender equity. The girls felt that they had also the support of
the intermediate teachers and that gender equity remained a feature of the
classroom. It could of course be argued that the ways in which these girls
constantly had to defend themselves were stressful and unhelpful. However,
girls who have managed to compete and win – as these girls had done – have
learnt not to lose in other competitive contexts. When they become adults,
their previous experience of competition will, it is hoped, aid them in any
competition with male colleagues.

Lisbeth's girls also seem to have gained, despite the fact that Lisbeth
tended to be more lenient towards the boys. It seems as if these largely
middle-class girls became motivated by the responsibility Lisbeth demanded
from them. They seemed to gain yet more when Anders later used their ways
of acting and relating to each other to show boys a good example of how
they should behave. It did not seem to matter that there were moments when
Anders used their caring qualities and pushed them into what we call the
maternal nurturance trap, or that Lars tried to challenge their achievements
at the end of the project. The girls entered the upper levels of schooling with
confidence in their capabilities and with a belief that equal relationships
with men will be vital when they grow up.

Lina and Siv agreed that their joint approach with the pupils should be implicit rather than explicit. Their classrooms were, in fact, the most contradictory and therefore the most difficult to understand. According to our observation notes and to the teachers' observations, the pupils seemed fond of each other and treated each other with respect and comradeship. There were no similar experiences of friendship between pupils in the other classes. It could therefore be argued that Lina and Siv had the greatest success in creating equal relationships between the pupils.

However, as we have seen, data can be contradictory. In interviews and written work, the girls, especially Siv's older girls, had complaints about the boys' apparent need to be superior in the classroom, and Lina's younger girls used the most traditional female stereotypes regarding their future family lives. It might therefore be argued that not being open about gender risks the reoccurrence or maintenance of dominant male norms. It might also be argued that 'calm' classrooms are not necessarily equal classrooms. The calmness could be explained by the fact that conventional and unequal gender patterns have never been challenged.

There are, however, data from the classrooms that again somewhat contradict these arguments. Lina's girls' accounts of traditional gender relations, in their essays about the future, were very different from the boys' accounts in theirs. The older girls' complaints about Siv's implicit and unclear pedagogy and Siv's resistance to them did not really seem to oppress the girls. On the contrary, the paradox arose that the girls' ability to reflect and challenge grew, and in this context the boys were generally supportive of the girls. Siv's resistance seemed to strengthen the solidarity between girls and boys in the classroom.

Another reason why the girls maintained claims for greater equality was the male teachers' support. All the male teachers said they felt comfortable in Siv's classroom, and they seemed to succeed in building good relationships with both girls and boys. We therefore suggest that, in a competitive masculine context, such as that which surrounded the school, male teachers working for gender equity are of great importance. However, it would be wrong to give the male teachers the entire credit for the good relationships between girls and boys. The solidarity between girls and boys would probably not have been established without Siv's strong commitment, during single-sex sessions with the boys, to supporting a softer masculinity, sensitive to people's feelings. It might also be argued that Siv's way of drawing on the general goodwill in the class facilitated solidarity between girls and boys. Our views that moments of normalization simultaneously produce moments of equity and vice versa have emerged most visibly from Lina's and Siv's pedagogy.

If the girls seemed to have gained, in one way or another, from this action research project, what about the boys? In Siv's classroom at intermediate level, Lina's former boys developed a masculinity that could be described as both sensitive and competitive. They were sensitive and loyal in relation to their female classmates and competitive when confronted by sport activities. In this competitive context, Siv's boys managed to combine the two without too much difficulty. They were respected by teachers as well as by the girls and by the other boys in the project. This was not the case for Eva's and Helena's boys. They did not successfully incorporate both elements. They kept on attaching too much importance to competition, especially since the girls were not willing to give up what they had achieved during their years with Eva. There seemed, however, to be some evidence that the boys gained from the gender equity pedagogy. According to their essays, they seemed not to hold stereotyped conceptions of women as carers in the family. The boys indicated that they were prepared to take care of themselves when adults and were confident that they could do so.

The boys who seemed to have gained least in this context where those in Lisbeth's and Anders's classes. It might be argued that Lisbeth's way of demonstrating her female moral superiority and of being too lenient to the boys seemed to generate in these middle-class boys a form of helplessness. In this context, as the girls became more mature and successful compared to the girls in other classes, the boys became more immature and helpless compared to the boys in other classes. The boys seemed to give up their struggle to achieve a dominant position in relation to the girls. Instead they let the girls set the tone and adapted themselves to the girls' norms. To start with they expressed satisfaction with this. They liked to play non-competitive games and they did not seem to mind receiving assistance with their schoolwork from the girls. They also expressed satisfaction with Anders, who supported the way they fitted in with the girls. The change occurred at the age of 12 or 13, when they realized that their status was too low at the school. Moreover, they did not seem to fit in with the competitive masculine discourse of the neighbourhood. Should we then draw the conclusion that these boys were the losers in the project? At the end of their schooling, most of these boys are likely to leave the neighbourhood for a job or for further education. How they will use their experiences of the gender project is not clear at present. However, it is likely that the ability to be sensitive to females in their private and public lives will be a great advantage and also will offer a contribution to the maintenance of gender equality.

Epilogue

As we have seen, action research for gender equity in this fairly standard middle-class environment took different forms in different classrooms, but, despite these differences, power was embodied in each of the project classrooms. We suggest that this will be the case in every context where a struggle for change is taking place. Each strategy for change therefore has the potential for danger. However, each strategy also has a potential for achieving positive changes towards, say, gender equity.

As mentioned above, in this era, which lies between the modern and the postmodern, the economy has become increasingly global. Market forces become increasingly influential in individual countries and states, and may also influence school systems and school policies. By naming these tendencies as patriarchal capitalism, we can also refer to the concept of moments of global normalization. The norm of the market does not support solidarity among individuals (as pupils or workers) or care work. Instead, it stresses competition and the survival of the fittest. In such contexts unpaid work and caring become a drawback for individuals. It seems as if Sweden is shifting to adopt the norms of the market, since care work is no longer explicitly stressed in Swedish school policy documents. However, this does not mean that those duties have disappeared. Every day and in various contexts, children have to be cared for in the home. Partial state funding of care workers at home has been seriously discussed as a possible new solution to the needs of people living in Sweden.

If care workers or servants now replace mothers and fathers in the home, will this constitute a new form of normalization, since most care workers will probably be women? If this is the case, who will take care of the children? Who will take care of home life? Such an analysis will also make visible how the boundaries between contextual discursive race and class relations are created. Is the modern conception of equality losing ground at a global level?

As long as we believe in a modern vision of equity, as long as gender exists and as long as there are unequal power relations between the sexes, there is a need for the implementation of gender equity pedagogy in classrooms. As long as gender equity pedagogy is needed in schools, action research can offer helpful tools for inquiry, exploration and development for teachers and pupils in their classrooms. To challenge and undermine the male norm, different groups in different contexts will need to come together, to try to go beyond ingrained gender discourses. They will need to create a diversity of new practices and new symbols. If that occurs, the value of different action research projects will be even greater, not just in Sweden but throughout the world.

Appendix 1:
Gender structures in Sweden

The Swedish public day care system, which dates back to the 1960s, expanded rapidly during the 1970s in parallel with increasing female participation in the labour force. Public childcare has been financed by large government subsidies and only to a minor degree by parents' fees, and is available for parents who study or are employed for at least 20 hours per week. In the 1980s the day care field was opened to private and quasi-market solutions. However, the majority of children are still taken care of in public childcare institutions (Oláh 1998).

Sweden has one of the world's highest percentages of women in the workforce. However, the fact that women work part-time to a greater degree than men suggests that women also largely take responsibility for unpaid work and family duties. During the 1970s the number of women working long part-time (20–35 hours a week) increased, and during the 1980s full-time work (40 hours a week) also increased. During the same period the number of males working full-time decreased and the number of those working part-time increased, but there were still big differences between women and men concerning full-time work. At the beginning of the 1990s unemployment increased for both women and men. In 1995, 80 per cent of women aged from 20 to 64, compared to 85 per cent of men, were in the labour force. Forty-five per cent of Swedish women worked full-time, 25 per cent long part-time and 4 per cent short part-time; 5 per cent of women were unemployed. Seventy-one per cent of Swedish men worked full-time, 5 per cent long part-time and 2 per cent short part-time, with 7 per cent unemployed (Swedish Statistics 1996).

Despite the high participation of women in the labour force, Sweden has one of the most sex-segregated labour markets. Women are better educated than men, but they are educated in undervalued and low paid fields, such as education, nursing, services and administration. The higher the salary, the more likely is an occupation to be male dominated. Women have a higher average salary in only five of 98 occupations. One in four Swedish men gets a salary of more than SEK 20,000 per month, while only one in ten Swedish women earns the same (*Dagens Nyheter* 29 March 1998).

A cross-national study conducted by Olin Wright *et al*. (1995) in the USA, Canada, the UK, Australia, Sweden, Norway and Japan confirmed that Sweden, together with Norway, has one of the largest gender gaps in workplace authority. This relatively large gender gap in workplace authority in the social democratic Scandinavian countries is explained as a by-product of the relatively low priority placed on the liberal goals of individual competition and achievement versus more communal benefits. A women's movement embedded in a social democratic political culture, as is the case in Sweden, could be expected to be less concerned with labour market mechanisms and more concerned with state interventions that directly provide services and resources that enhance women's welfare, such as parental leave, maternal health care, childcare services and child allowances (Olin Wright *et al*. 1995). However, female political representation has increased, and became the highest in the world by the mid-1990s. Representation at the top levels in politics became, during the 1990s, equal regarding the sexes. Fifty per cent of all top officials in ministries and 44 per cent of all Members of Parliamentary Committees are women (Swedish Statistics 1996).

Insurance protection has not, as in other countries, been limited to the full-time employed only (Oláh 1998). Sweden has the Western world's most generous provisions for paid parental leave. The 1995 parental insurance regulation states that one month of the cash benefit must be used by the mother and one month by the father, in 'dad's month'. Payment covers 90 per cent of the parent's current wage. The remaining 390 days can be used by either parent; for 300 days the benefit is paid at the rate of 80 per cent of the parental wage, followed by 90 days with a minimum payment. In 1993, 74 per cent of women but only 27 per cent of men used the cash benefit. If a child under 12 years needs to be taken care of because of, for example, illness, or if the person who takes care of the child becomes ill, there is a possibility of getting a temporary cash benefit. Temporary cash benefit can be transferred from the parents to any other person who stays home from work to care for the child. In 1990, the temporary cash benefit period increased to 120 days per child (under 12 years) per year. In 1993, the temporary cash benefit was used by 41 per cent of men and 59 per cent of women (Swedish Statistics 1995).

However, in 1996 payments for the 'dad's month' were reduced from 90 to 85 per cent of the wage, and cash benefits for the remaining 300 days from 80 to 75 per cent. Family allowances were reduced from SEK 750 for each child to SEK 640 (Swedish Statistics 1996). The Swedish pension system is also declining. The universal coverage of the whole population, whether they have been in paid or unpaid work, is a flat-rate basic pension called 'the people's pension'. In addition to this pension to ensure a proper living standard for everyone, there has been a national supplementary pension (the so-called

ATP). The ATP has been determined by the fifteen best earnings years in a 30-year employment period. Since women work part-time more often than men, especially while the family has pre-school children, this system is especially favourable to women. However, according to a new pension programme, there should be a more direct connection between lifetime salary and pension level. This new programme favours full-time employment and overtime work for a long period; it does not favour those women and men who spend time shouldering domestic responsibilities in accordance with the core of gender equality rhetoric in Sweden.

A current debate in Sweden is connected with that question. The debate is about whether or not the state should partly finance salaries for domestic help in families. The arguments for such a solution have been borrowed from gender equality rhetoric in paid work. Having domestic help gives both women and men an equal chance to compete on the labour market and to take part in political work. This new service area could also solve the problem of increasing unemployment, especially since there are cuts in subsidies to the public sector and a lot of people working there are losing their jobs. In an opinion poll, 54 per cent Swedes (54 per cent males and 53 per cent females) agreed with the suggestion of state part funded home help. Non-socialist voters were most affirmative, but 40 per cent of social democrats agreed with paying for domestic help if the state subsidizes half the costs (*Västerbottens kuriren* 28 March 1998).

Teaching has become increasingly dominated by women. Of all the teachers in compulsory schools during the school year 1996/7 only 28 per cent were male. The corresponding figure in 1985/6 was 32 per cent. However, the most significant increase in women can be seen among head-teachers. During the past ten years the proportion of female headteachers has increased from 10 to 55 per cent (Swedish Statistics 1997). However, this increase has taken place during a period of less special education, fewer teachers, less money in schools and less money in families, especially in single parent (mainly mothers) families (Nilsson 1998). The female head-teachers are administrating a decline in compulsory schools. The increase in the number of female heads in schools, as mentioned above, is mirrored in other parts of the public sector. According to Holmberg (1997), the administration of the declining welfare state by women is an increasingly common picture in the public sector today.

The educational attainment of the Swedish population has grown rapidly during the postwar period. Upper secondary education has changed from being the privilege of a minority to being the norm for most young people. In 1996, only a quarter of the adult population between the ages of 25 and 64 years had only lower secondary education as their highest level of education. Half the population had completed upper secondary education and the remaining quarter had completed higher education. Upper secondary school is voluntary but there are practically no pupils from compulsory school who do not apply. Upper secondary schools have the capacity to admit more pupils than the total number of compulsory school leavers. Since 1992, there have been gradual changes in order to create schools with only three-year programmes and thereby make all upper secondary school leavers eligible for studies at university or higher education college. Girls and boys are on average distributed almost equally in the first year of upper secondary school. However, when one looks at the programmes separately, gender differences are obvious, and they essentially follow the Swedish tradition, as well as the tradition in other countries. That is, the girls dominate programmes that relate to nursing, care and arts, while the boys heavily dominate programmes focused on technology and physics.

Marks are not awarded until the first term in year 8 in compulsory school. The girls are doing well at school. In spring 1996 in the ninth grade, girls had better average marks than boys in all subjects, with the exception of physical education and technology. In upper secondary school the girls achieved the highest average marks on all lines and programmes and girls completing the natural science programme achieved the highest average mark. There has been discussion as to whether the assessments are fair or not, and since 1991 there has been an alternative way to enter higher education, which appears to favour boys. A university aptitude test has been developed and is used as an alternative method of selection to higher education, in addition to applicants' marks. The applicant can choose whether he or she wants to do the test. Men on average have consistently achieved better results than women in these university aptitude tests.

Students receive help to finance their university studies in the form of a non-repayable grant plus a larger loan from central government. The percentage of university entrants increased heavily between 1991 and 1995, from 19 to 28 per cent of the relevant age cohort. However, the regional distribution of people with higher education is uneven. Counties containing university have higher rates than other counties. There are even bigger differences between the municipalities: in many big city areas well over 20 per cent of the population have a university, compared with 4 per cent in many of the rural municipalities. The education level of parents has a large impact on university recruitment. Fifty-nine per cent of entrants, 37 per cent have parents with less than three years' higher education and 13 per cent have parents with compulsory education only. Seven years after completing compulsory school education, 16 per cent of young people with a parent born abroad have a university degree or are in higher education. The corresponding figure among young people with parents born in Sweden is 23 per cent.

The traditional gender differences in subject studied remain intact. Women dominate the fields of teaching and health-related science (77 and 89 per cent respectively), while men dominate the fields of technology/natural sciences (73 per cent) and agriculture/forestry (64 per cent). The field that has the least difference between the sexes is medicine/dentistry. Far more women than men pass undergraduate studies, but just 30 per cent of doctorate and licentiate degrees are awarded to women. The teaching and research staff in state universities and university colleges and county administered colleges of health science are dominated by men. Of professors and senior lecturers, 91 and 75 per cent respectively are men (Swedish Statistics 1997).

Although Sweden (together with the other Nordic countries) has one of the highest rates of gender equity in the world, it is obvious that segregation and hierarchy still permeate higher education, as well as paid and unpaid work, in Sweden.

Appendix 2:
Curriculum for gender equity:
the teachers' voices

We now outline our policy regarding gender equity. Given that gender is a social and cultural construction, gender division in single-sex groups should not be regarded as an aim but as a method to reach the goal of gender equity stressed in the national curriculum. By assigning about a quarter of the total amount of time to gender-sensitive content in single-sex groups, we hope that the pupils will come together on more equal terms in mixed-gender groups. However, we are aware that segregation in single-sex groups may reinforce traditional gender dichotomies and that old gender patterns can very easily emerge in new costumes. We will try to be sensitive to such normalizing tendencies and hope to counteract them with suitable strategies.

Our policy relates directly to the three foundations of the concept of gender equity. We end by describing how we work to encourage the pupils' self-confidence.

Equity in paid work

Equity between the sexes means that women and men share the same rights, responsibilities and opportunities to pursue work which provides economic independence. This becomes a question of developing forms, methods and content in a gender-sensitive pedagogy aimed at breaking the segregation and hierarchy in the labour market and in higher education.

Technology (7–10 year age group)

The aim is to strengthen girls' self-confidence so that they will feel familiar within the subject of technology, which is charged with male symbolism. We have observed that in coed classes boys 'take over' the laboratory work at the cost of girls. At the junior level they are taught by a female teacher. The pupils thus get a female role model. During the first two grades the teaching is carried out in single-sex groups, so that girls can perform their laboratory work and reflect on the different steps of the course at their own pace. Coed classes are used during the third grade, but the laboratory experiments are still performed in smaller single-sex groups. The aim is to make boys aware of the fact that girls can handle problems within a traditionally male area, and to make girls aware of the fact that their ways of dealing with technology are just as valid as those of boys.

General science and computer knowledge (10–13 year age group)

The teaching proceeds at intermediate level with the same aim as above, in both single-sex and coed groups, in the subjects of chemistry, physics, biology, computing and technology. These subjects are taught by both female and male teachers. Thus the pupils encounter both male and female teachers in traditionally male subjects.

Girls play rock music (10–13 year age group)

Hard rock is often connected with masculinity. The aim is to train girls, by playing rock in single-sex groups, to act together in areas other than the traditionally female. If girls learn to perform in this masculine area, we hope they will get the courage to try other areas connected with men's domains. We hope this can be transferred to, for example, choice of studies and choice of professions.

Visiting parents' places of work (all ages)

With parents we arrange for boys to visit traditional women's places of work and, for girls to visit men's places of work. The aim is to give boys an insight into and knowledge of work dominated by women and to give girls an insight into and knowledge of work dominated by men. Parents who work in professions that are not gender traditional are specially invited to school for further discussions. This year a male nurse and a female bus driver were invited.

Work experience scheme (10–13 year age group)

The aim of this activity is to give the pupils an insight into the different kinds of work that take place in the school. For one week, in some lessons each day, the pupils accompany and work together with some of the staff. The pupils do not have a free choice of work. They draw lots, since their choices are often gender-stereotyped.

Visits from elderly people (all ages)

Older people are invited to the school to answer the question 'What was life like in this area in the past?' The aim is to get a local historical and cultural explanation of the gender division in work in this area yesterday and today.

Equity in caring for children and the home

Equity between the sexes means that women and men share the same rights, responsibilities and opportunities to care for children and home. This becomes a question of developing forms, methods and content in a gender-sensitive pedagogy aimed at breaking the segregation and hierarchy in unpaid work. It also deals with the development of skills in perspective shifts, e.g. empathy.

Care work (7–10 year age group)

The aim is that both boys and girls will, through practical work, obtain knowledge about care work, including some basic knowledge of textile craft, home economics and the study of children and childhood. The principal aim is to strengthen boys' self-confidence within a subject and area charged with femininity. It is hoped that their curiosity and interest will be awakened, so that they can do care work on their own initiative and put questions about the division of labour to other members of the family. The pupils will learn that unpaid work has to be carried out by someone every day. Care work is based on a different logic from paid work. The more care work you do the more invisible it becomes. The less you do the more visible it becomes. This care work teaching is strongly inspired by the Norwegian project led by Professor Hildur Ve.

In order to encourage a feeling of caring, especially among the boys, the pupils sew their own mascots. They also produce the necessary accessories, such as clothes and a bed. The mascots are used in different role plays. In order to get real-life insights into parenthood a father or a mother is invited to school with their baby. The aim is to give the pupils a basic idea as to how to take care of a baby. We also inform the pupils about parents' rights when a child is born: for example, legislation on maternity and parental leave. Care for the clothes and basic cooking are also included in care work teaching.

We have observed that in coed classes girls 'take over' the care work at the cost of boys. We therefore use single-sex groups during the first two years, so that boys can do their care work and reflect on the various issues raised by the course at their own pace. Coed classes are used during the third grade, but the work is still done in smaller sex-segregated groups. The aim is to make girls aware of the fact that boys can handle problems within a symbolic female area, and to make boys aware that their ways of dealing with care work are every bit as valuable as those of the girls.

Home Economics (10–13 year age group)

After a break during the fourth grade, the pupils have home economics on the schedule again in the fifth grade. The pupils are taught by a male teacher. The aim is to give the pupils a male role model within an area connected with femininity. The pupils learn cooking, care of clothes and other chores, with the same aim as above. The teaching is carried out in single-sex groups again, since experience showed that the boys tended to mess around in coed groups. Parents are involved and are asked to encourage pupils to carry out basic tasks at home: for example, making beds, cleaning floors washing clothes and watering house plants.

Craft (10–13 year age group)

One of the aims of craft (textile craft and woodwork and metalwork) is to enable everyone to perform tasks in peace and quiet. For the same reasons as in home economics the pupils are educated in single-sex groups, again by two craft teachers. Thus boys will be able to practise work connected with femininity, such as sewing, needlework and knitting, without asking the girls for help and girls will be able to practice work connected with masculinity such as handling machines and tools, without asking the boys for help. Ridiculing is also avoided.

Godfathers' and godmothers' activities (all ages)

The aim of these activities, at intermediate level, is to teach both girls and boys how to take care of a younger pupil at junior level. Each pupil at junior level gets a godmother or a godfather from the intermediate level. The older children can, for example, help the younger children to write, read their own stories to them or help them with their homework. They also coach the younger children in basketball, dancing and canoeing, they organize excursions, perform musicals and have parties together. The main aim is to train boys as well as girls to exchange perspectives and to teach them empathy. The younger pupils get role models who are responsible for their needs.

'Talk about feelings' (all ages)

Boys in this school often find it difficult to express feelings in words. The aim is to enable the boys to express their feelings and to settle conflicts without scuffles.

Sex education (10–13 year age group)

In the sixth grade the pupils go camping in single-sex groups for two days. The aim is to give the pupils information about sexuality, coexistence and drugs, and to discuss these issues. A lot of time is devoted to making the pupils aware of their own values and to motivating different positions concerning sexuality and cohabitation. The girls go with their female teachers and with other female members of staff – the school nurse, the school welfare officer and the school psychologist – to discuss personal relationships and females' rights to master their own bodies. The boys go with their male teachers and with other male members of staff – the school medical officer and the school clergyman – to discuss and to try to replace the distorted picture of love that the boys might have received from porn films with a more dignified and honest picture of love and personal relationships.

Equity in politics, unions and other societal activities

Equity in politics means that women and men share the same rights, responsibilities and opportunities to participate in politics, unions and other societal activities. This becomes a question of developing forms, methods and content in a gender-sensitive pedagogy, further aiming at breaking segregation and hierarchies relating to participation in different political activities. It also deals with learning to express one's opinions and having the courage to participate in public debates with people who have other opinions. The main aim is to educate girls and boys for citizenship in democracies.

Daily news (all ages)

In order to prepare girls, in particular, for public debates, the daily news presented in newspapers and other media is discussed in single-sex groups. The aim of using single-sex groups is to train girls not to hand over responsibility for public debate and political events to boys. In the year in which Sweden entered the European Union, a lot of time was devoted to the referendum concerning membership of the European Union and to general elections in Sweden.

Rostrum or speaker's corner (7–10 year age group)

The pupils sit in front of the class and tell the others something. The aim is to teach them how to be heard, how to speak up and how to argue for or against something.

Vocabulary and word comprehension (10–13 year age group)

Public debates often include 'difficult' words. We teach words used in, for example, politics and economy. The aim is to give all pupils a vocabulary that is large enough for participation in public debates.

Negotiations (10–13 year age group)

The aim is to make the pupils aware of current gender equity questions and different laws within this area. The pupils practise preparing and carrying out negotiations. The valuation of male and female occupations is one important question. These negotiations are followed up by gender-conscious discussions.

Ruling techniques (all ages)

The aim is to make the pupils aware of Berit Ås's concept of five ruling techniques. If you can make them visible you can also handle them. Pupils at intermediate level write short plays on themes taken from everyday life, illustrating various ruling techniques. The older pupils perform these plays for the younger pupils, and the performances are followed up with discussions on how to treat these ruling techniques and how to change these circumstances.

Self-confidence

In order to bridge gender divisions and to break hierarchies, to give space as well as to claim space, boys and girls must have self-confidence. The aim is that the pupils should feel proud of themselves and learn in what situations their qualities will be useful. However, the main aim is to strengthen their undeveloped faculties. If necessary, single-sex groups are used.

Swedish (all ages)

From a general point of view, the ability to write differs between the sexes in this school. The girls write very well compared with the boys, whose ability tends to be more modest. On the other hand, boys have no problem in expressing themselves orally. Girls are less spontaneous, and are not very willing to speak in public unless they are well prepared. In the segregated groups girls and boys get a profiled education. Girls are encouraged to speak up in public and boys are taught to develop their writing and to make perspective shifts.

English (10–13 year age group)

As for Swedish.

Creative activities (7–10 year age group)

The pupils practise games, dancing and educational drama. The aim is to join and to remove barriers between boys' and girls' different forms of expressing themselves in different educational creative activities. During the first two grades single-sex groups are used, but in the third grade the pupils perform creative activities together. The aim is to make girls and boys aware of the fact that activities can be performed in different but equally valuable ways and that problems can be solved in a variety of different ways. In dancing and games the children learn to appreciate working together. These activities also train children's coordination and dexterity, as well as their brains and bodies.

Physical education (10–13 year age group)

Physical education has often been on boys' terms in the sixth grade in this school. A lot of girls try to avoid coed physical lessons in this school and become passive. In order to encourage girls to be more active during the lessons, physical education is carried out in single-sex groups on girls' terms.

School choir (10–13 year age group)

The school has both a girls' choir and a boys' choir. The rock groups mentioned above emanate from these choirs. Girls and boys have the opportunity to influence their own repertory. The need for this increases when boys' voices are breaking. The music teacher experienced a big influx of boys to the choir when he started to teach in single-sex groups. Choirs are symbolically connected with femininity, but when the boys were able to influence their repertory with, for example, more rap, they came in flocks. In single-sex groups boys and girls also have the courage to take up forms of expression symbolically connected with the other sex. Boys still start traditional hard rock groups, but they do not leave the boys' choir. Girls usually join the choir, but they also start rock groups and learn to play both the drums and the guitar.

The choirs perform a show every year. To be on stage, to perform and to be at the centre of attention are other ways of reaching self-confidence. The musical this year is about an imaginary trip to developing countries. The aim is to make the pupils aware of imperialistic tendencies and unequal relations between developed and developing countries, but the pupils also carry out research in order to learn more about differences between boys and girls in these countries.

References

Adelman, C. (1993) Kurt Lewin and the origins of action research, *Educational Action Research*, 1(1): 7–23.

Altrichter, H. (1993) *Teachers Investigate Their Work: An Introduction to the Methods of Action Research*. London: Routledge.

Arnesen, A.-L. (ed.) (1995) *Gender and Equality as Quality in School and Teacher Education*. Oslo: Oslo College School of Education.

Ås, B. (1982) *Kvinnor tillsammans. Handbok i frigörelse*. (Women Together. Handbook in Emancipation.) Malmö: Gidlunds.

Banks, O. (1981) *Faces of Feminism: A Study of Feminism as a Social Movement*. Oxford: Martin Robertson.

Berge, B.-M. (1992) Gå i lära till lärare – en grupp kvinnors och en grupp mäns inskolning i slöjdläraryrket. (Craft teachers as spearheads for an equal society? A study of female and male future craft teachers and of the school subject craft in Swedish compulsory school.) Doctoral thesis, Umeå University Department of Education.

Berge, B.-M. (1997) Steering of teachers' work – lessons from an action research project in Sweden, *Teacher Education and Research in Umeå*, 2: 7–22.

Björkly, W. and Hernes, I. (1993) *Det er artig att vaere grei*. (It's good to be OK.) Tromsö: Krokelvdal Skole.

Butler, J. (1990) *Gender Trouble: Feminism and the Subversion of Identity*. New York: Routledge.

Chisholm, L. A. and Holland, J. (1986) Girls and occupational choice: anti-sexism in action in a curriculum project, *British Journal of Sociology of Education*, 7(4): 353–65.

Davies, B. (1997) The subject of post-structuralism: a reply to Alison Jones, *Gender and Education*, 9(3): 271–83.

Dewey, J. (1929) *The Quest for Certainty*. New York: Perigee (1980 edition).

Dewey, J. (1958) *Experiences and Nature*, 2nd edn. New York: Dover.

Elliott, J. (1991) *Action Research for Educational Change*. Buckingham: Open University Press.

Ellsworth, E. (1989) Why doesn't this feel empowering? Working through the repressive myths of critical pedagogy, in C. Luke and J. Gore (eds) *Feminisms and Critical Pedagogy*. New York: Routledge.

Florin, C. and Nilsson, B. (1997) 'Something in the nature of a bloodless revolution.'

How new gender relations became 'equal status policy' in Sweden in the 1960s and 1970s. Paper presented to SCASS, Uppsala University, 28 May.

Forsberg, U. (1998) Jämställdhetspedagogik – en sammanställning av aktions-forskningsprojekt. (Gender equity pedagogy – a compilation of action research projects.) *Educational Reports*, Department of Education, Umeå University, no. 55.

Foucault, M. (1980) Truth and power, in C. Gordon (ed.) *Power/Knowledge: Selected Interviews and Other Writings 1972–1977*. New York: Pantheon Books.

Foucault, M. (1983) The subject and power, in H. L. Dreyfus and P. Rabinow (eds) *Michel Foucault: Beyond Structuralism and Hermeneutics*, 2nd edn. Chicago: University of Chicago Press.

Freeman, J. G. (1996) An exploratory study of a gender equity program for secondary school students, *Gender and Education*, 8(3): 289–300.

Frith, R. and Mahony, P. (eds) (1994) *Promoting Quality and Equality in Schools*. London: Fulton Publishers.

Gore, J. (1990) What we can do for you! What can 'we' do for 'you'? Struggling over empowerment in critical and feminist pedagogy, in C. Luke and J. Gore (eds) *Feminisms and Critical Pedagogy*. New York: Routledge.

Griffiths, M. and Davies, C. (1993) Learning to learn. Action research from an equal opportunities perspective in a junior school, *British Educational Research Journal*, 19(1): 43–58.

Gunneriussen, W. (1997) Å forstå det moderne. Rapport. Samfunnsvitenskapelig Fakultet, Universitetet i Tromsø.

Harding, S. (1986) *The Science Question in Feminism*. Ithaca, NY: Cornell University Press.

Harding, S. (1991) *Whose Science? Whose Knowledge? Thinking from Women's Lives*. Buckingham: Open University Press.

Heldke, L. (1989) John Dewey and Evelyn Fox Keller: a shared epistemological tradition. In N. Tuana (ed.) *Feminism and Science*. Bloomington: Indiana University Press.

Hernes, G. (1975) *Makt og avmakt*. Oslo: Universitetsforlaget.

Hollingsworth, S. (1994) Feminist pedagogy in the research class: an example of teacher research, *Educational Action Research*, 2(1): 49–70.

Hollingsworth, S. (1997) *International Action Research: A Casebook for Educational Reform*. London: Falmer Press.

Holmberg, Carin (1997) Den ömma bödeln. Kvinnliga ledare i åtstramningstider. (The caring executioner. Female leaders during periods of austerity.) *SOU*, 83: 147–77.

Jaggar, A. (1983) *Feminist Politics and Human Nature*. Totowa, NJ: Rowman and Allanheld.

Joas, H. (1993) *Pragmatism and Social Theory*. Chicago: University of Chicago Press.

Jones, A. (1997) Teaching post-structuralist feminist theory in education: student resistances, *Gender and Education*, 9(3): 261–9.

Kalleberg, R. (1991) A constructive turn in sociology, *Studies of Higher Education* (Oslo), autumn.

Kalleberg, R. (1992) Konstruktiv samfunnsvitenskap. En fagteoretisk plassering av 'aksjonsforskning'. (Constructive social science. A theoretical disciplinary positioning of 'action research'.) Rapport no. 24, Institutt for sosiologi, Universitetet i Oslo.

Keller, E. F. (1985) *Reflections on Gender and Science.* New Haven, CT: Yale University Press.

Kenway, J., Willis, S., Blackmore, J. and Rennie, L. (1993) Learning from girls: what can girls teach feminist teachers? in L. Yates (ed.) *Feminism and Education.* Melbourne: La Trobe University Press.

Kochenberger-Stroeher, S. (1994) Cherry Creek School District, Englewood, CO: sixteen kindergartners' gender-related views of careers, *Elementary School Journal,* 95(1): 95–103.

Kruse, A.-M. (1992) '. . . We have learnt not to sit back, twiddle our thumbs and let them take over.' Single-sex settings and the development of a pedagogy for girls and a pedagogy for boys in Danish schools, *Gender and Education,* 4(1/2): 81–103.

Ladson-Billings, G. (1994) *The Dream Keepers: Successful Teachers of African American Children.* San Fransisco: Jossey-Bass.

Läroplan för grundskolan (1962) Swedish National Curriculum. Stockholm: Skolöverstyrelsen.

Läroplan för grundskolan (1969) Swedish National Curriculum. Stockholm: Liber.

Läroplan för grundskolan (1980) Swedish National Curriculum. Stockholm: Liber.

Lather, P. (1991) *Getting Smart: Feminist Research and Pedagogy with/in the Postmodern.* New York: Routledge.

Leeming, P. (1991) Action research on gender issues, *National Union of Teachers Education Review,* 5, 1.

Lewin, K. (ed.) (1948) *Resolving Social Conflicts.* New York.

Lewis, M. (1990) Interrupting partriachy: politics, resistance and transformation in the feminist classroom, in C. Luke and J. Gore (eds) *Feminisms and Critical Pedagogy.* New York: Routledge.

Lock, R. S. and Minarik, L. T. (1997) Gender equity in an elementary classroom: the power of praxis in action research, in S. Hollingsworth (ed.) *International Action Research: A Casebook for Educational Reform.* London: Falmer Press.

Luke, C. and Gore, J. (eds) (1992) *Feminisms and Critical Pedagogy.* New York: Routledge.

Miller, J. (1990) *Creating Spaces and Finding Voices. Teachers Collaborating for Empowerment.* New York: State University of New York Press.

Miller, J. B. (1982) Women and power. Work in Progress, Stone Center for Developmental Services and Studies, Wellesley College, No. 82–01.

Nationell kvalitetsgranskning av skolan (1998) Rapport från Skolverket, Stockholm.

Neal, M. (1991) Implementing equal opportunity in a boys' secondary school, in P. Lomax (ed.), *Managing Better Schools and Colleges: Bera Dialogues 5.* Clevedon: Multilingual Matters.

Nicholas, M. (1991) Gender dynamics and support teaching: an action research experiment in a multi-ethnic middle school, in P. Lomax (ed.) *Managing Better Schools and Colleges: BERA Dialogues 5.* Clevedon: Multilingual Matters.

Nilsson, I. (1998) Social justice and welfare state in decline. Paper presented to AERA Annual Meeting, San Diego, 13–17 April.

Noffke, S. E. (1997) Themes and tensions in US action research: towards historical analysis, in S. Hollingsworth (ed.) *International Action Research: A Casebook for Educational Reform.* London: Falmer Press.

Noffke, S. E. and Brennan, M. (1997) Reconstructing the politics of action in action research, in S. Hollingsworth (ed.) *International Action Research: A Casebook for Educational Reform*. London: Falmer Press.

Olafsdottir, Marga Paula (1993) Hjalli en ovanlig lekskola. Könsindelning ger jämlikhet – könsintegrering skapar orättvisa. (Hjalli, an unusual kindergarten. Single-sex groups create equality – sex-integrated groups create unequality.) *Skolen i Norden*, 3.

Oláh, L. S. (1998) Sweden, the middle way: a feminist approach, *European Journal of Women's Studies*, 5: 47–67.

Orner, M. (1992) Interrupting the calls for student voice in 'liberatory' education: a feminist poststructuralist perspective, in C. Luke and J. Gore (eds) *Feminisms and Critical Pedagogy*. New York: Routledge.

Parker, L. H. and Rennie, L. R. (1995) *For the Sake of the Girls? Final Report of the Western Australian Single-sex Education Pilot Project 1993–1994*. Perth, Western Australia: Curtin University of Technology.

Parsons, T. (1937) *The Structure of Social Action*. Glencoe, IL: The Free Press.

Pateman, C. (1989) *The Sexual Contract*. Cambridge: Polity Press.

Pohl, P. (1991) *Malins kung Gurra*. Simrishamn: Raben and Sjögren.

Putnam, Hilary (1994) *Words and Life*. Cambridge, MA: Harvard University Press.

Slee, R., Weiner, G. and Tomlinson, S. (eds) (1998) *School Effectiveness for Whom? Challenges to the School Effectiveness and the School Improvement Movement*. London: Falmer Press.

Spivak, G. C. (1993) *Outside in the Teaching Machine*. New York: Routledge.

Statens utdanningskontor i Hordaland (1992) Omsorgsfulle gutter og tekniske jenter – eller var det omvendt? (Caring boys and technical girls – or was it reversed?) Rapport fra likestillingsprosjektet 1–3 klasse.

Swedish Government Bill (1987/8) Om jämställdhetspolitik inför 90-talet. (About gender equity politics approaching the 1990s.) Proposition 1987/8: 105.

Swedish Government Bill (1993/4) Delad makt delat ansvar. (Shared power shared responsibility.) Proposition 1993/4: 147.

Swedish Government Bill (1994/5) Jämställdhet mellan kvinnor och män inom utbildningsområdet. (Equality between men and women within education.) Proposition 1994/5: 164.

Swedish Statistics (1995) *Women and Men in Sweden – Equality of the Sexes*. Stockholm: Swedish Statistics.

Swedish Statistics (1996) *Women and Men in Sweden – Equality of the Sexes*. Stockholm: Swedish Statistics.

Swedish Statistics (1997) *Education in Sweden*. Stockhom: Swedish Statistics.

Tabachnick, B. R. and Zeichner, K. M. (eds) (1991) *Issues and Practices in Inquiry-oriented Teacher Education*. London: Falmer Press.

Tiller, T. (1986) *Den Tenkende Skolen – Om Organisasionsutvikling og Aksjonslaering på Skolens Egne Premiser*. (The Reflective School – About Organizational Development and Action Learning on Schools' Own Premises.) Universitetsforlaget.

Tutchell, E. (ed.) (1990) *Dolls and Dungarees. Gender Issues in the Primary School Curriculum*. Buckingham: Open University Press.

Tuulenkari, L. (1995) ILONA-class: new opportunities for girls, in A.-L. Arnesen (ed.) *Gender and Equality as Quality in School and Teacher Education*. Oslo: Oslo College School of Education.

Vaage, S. (1998) Å ta andres perspektiv. Grunnlag for sosialisering og identitet. George Herbert Mead i utvalg. Stockholm: Abstrakt forlag.

Ve, H. (1992) Aktionsforskning och jämställdhetsarbete i skolan. (Action research and work for gender equality in school.) Kvinnovetenskaplig tidskrift, 3: 64–74.

Ve, H. (1995) On gender and equality in schools in late modernity: a feminist attitude towards poststructuralist viewpoints on society and education, in K. Reisby and K. Schnack (eds) What Can Curriculum Studies and Pedagogy Learn from Sociology Today? Studies in Educational Theory and Curriculum, Volume 16. Copenhagen: Royal Danish School of Educational Studies.

Ve, H. (1998) Education, social justice, individualization and citizenship rights: a feminist perspective. Paper presented to AERA Annual Meeting, San Diego, 13–17 April.

Walkerdine, V. (1986) Progressive pedagogy and political struggle, in C. Luke and J. Gore (eds) Feminisms and Critical Pedagogy. New York: Routledge.

Weiner, G. (1989) Professional self-knowledge versus social justice: a critical analysis of the teacher-researcher movement, British Educational Research Journal, 15: 41–51.

Weiner, G. (1990) Developing educational policy on gender in the primary school: the contributions of teachers in the United Kingdom, in G. Weiner (ed.) The Primary School and Equal Opportunities. London: Cassell.

Weiner, G. (1994) Feminisms in Education: An Introduction. Buckingham: Open University Press.

Weiner, G. (1997) Action research and social justice: some experiences of schools in the inner city, in S. Hollingsworth (ed.) International Action Research: A Casebook for Educational Reform. London: Falmer Press.

Weiner, G. (1998) Educational reform, gender and class in Britain: understanding shifts in discourses of social justice. Paper presented to AERA Annual Meeting, San Diego, 13–17 April.

Westblade, B. and Miller-Kenneth, J. (1989) Northern Territory gender-inclusive curriculum project – maths and science, years 4–7, Australian Science Teachers' Journal, 35(3): 93–5.

Wright Olin, E., Baxter, J. and Birkelund, G. E. (1995) The gender gap in workplace authority: a cross national study, American Sociological Review, 60: 407–35.

Young, I. M. (1990) Justice and the Politics of Difference. Princeton, NJ: Princeton University Press.

Index

EDUCATING MUSLIM GIRLS
SHIFTING DISCOURSES

Kaye Haw

- Do Muslim girls have access to equal educational opportunities in British schools?
- To what extent do issues of race and gender affect the education of Muslim girls?

This important book examines the relationships between teachers (often white and non-Muslim) and their female Muslim students in two single sex schools – one an urban comprehensive, the other a private Muslim school – and explores the ways in which these relationships are affected by different educational settings and experiences. The tensions between the twin priorities of equality and difference which shape feminist discourses in education are carefully analysed. The book begins by developing a theoretical framework which reflects current debates within feminism and post-structuralism in a coherent and accessible way to enable readers coming to these debates for the first time to develop a basic understanding. At the same time the book will serve to challenge the reader and can be seen as a springboard for those who wish to explore these theoretical debates further.

The book will be of interest to students and academics in the fields of women's studies, education, research methods and social studies.

Contents
Introduction – Part I: Contexts and themes: negotiating the maze – Framing the issues from the margins – Flash-backs-and-forth: re-searching the roots – Schooling for Muslim students in contemporary Britain – Gender, Islam and single-sex schooling – Part II: Re-searching the research: disentangling the dynamics – City State and Old Town High – Equality in difference? – The Nazrah story – Dancing with the discourses: re-searching the research – Glossary – References – Index.

224pp   0 335 19773 6 (Paperback)   0 335 19774 4 (Hardback)

EDUCATIONAL RESEARCH FOR SOCIAL JUSTICE
GETTING OFF THE FENCE

Morwenna Griffiths

This is a book for all researchers in educational settings whose research is motivated by considerations of justice, fairness and equity. It addresses questions such researchers have to face. Will a prior political or ethical commitment bias the research? How far can the ideas of empowerment or 'giving a voice' be realized? How can researchers who research communities to which they belong deal with the ethical issues of being both insider and outsider?

The book provides a set of principles for doing educational research for social justice. These are rooted in considerations of methodology, epistemology and power relations, and provide a framework for dealing with the practical issues of collaboration, ethics, bias, empowerment, voice, uncertain knowledge and reflexivity, at all stages of research from getting started to dissemination and taking responsibility as members of the wider community of educational researchers.

Theoretical arguments and the realities of practical research are brought together and interwoven. Thus the book will be helpful to all researchers, whether they are just beginning their first project, or whether they are already highly experienced. It will be of great value to research students in designing and writing up their theses and dissertations.

Contents
Part I: Introduction and context – Taking sides, getting change – Research for social justice? Some examples – Part II: Theoretical frameworks for practical purposes – Truths and methods – Facts and values: power/knowledge – Living with uncertainty in educational research – Educational research for social justice: a framework – Part III: Practical possibilities – Getting started: the research process – Getting justice: empowerment and voice – Better knowledge – Educational research at large – Appendix: Fair schools – References – Index.

176pp   0 335 19859 7 (Paperback)   0 335 19860 0 (Hardback)

FAILING BOYS?
ISSUES IN GENDER AND ACHIEVEMENT

Debbie Epstein, Jannette Elwood, Valerie Hey and Janet Maw

Failing Boys? Issues in Gender and Achievement challenges the widespread perception that all boys are underachieving at school. It raises the more important and critical questions of which boys? At what stage of education? And according to what criteria?

The issues surrounding boys' 'underachievement' have been at the centre of public debate about education and the raising of standards in recent years. Media and political responses to the 'problem of boys' have tended to be simplistic, partial, and owe more to 'quick fixes' than investigation and research. *Failing Boys?* provides a detailed and nuanced 'case study' of the issues in the UK, which will be of international relevance as the moral panic is a globalised one, taking place in diverse countries. The contributors to this book take seriously the issues of boys' 'underachievement' inside and outside school from a critical perspective which draws on the insights of previous feminist studies of education to illuminate the problems associated with the education of boys.

This will be a key text for educators, policy makers, students and teachers of education, sociology, gender studies and cultural studies and others interested in gender and achievement.

Contents
Part I: Boys' underachievement in context – Part II: Different constructions of the debate and its undercurrents – Part III: Boys, which boys? – Part IV: Curriculum, assessment and the debate

208pp   0 335 20238 1 (Paperback)   0 335 20239 X (Hardback)